Can't Learn, Won't Learn, Don't Care

Also available from Continuum

Handbook of Social, Emotional and Behavioural Difficulties –
Paul Cooper, Morag Hunter-Carsch, Rosemary Sage, Yonca
Tiknaz

ADHD (Second Edition) – Fintan J. O'Regan

Surviving and Succeeding in SEN – Fintan J. O'Regan

Getting the Buggers To Behave (Third Edition) – Sue Cowley

Managing Very Challenging Behaviour – Louisa Leaman

Managing Boys' Behaviour – Tabatha Rayment

Dos and Don'ts of Behaviour Management – Roger Dunn

Managing Behaviour in the Early Years – Janet Kay

Can't Learn, Won't Learn, Don't Care

Troubleshooting Challenging Behaviour

Fintan J. O'Regan, MA

continuum

Continuum International Publishing Group

The Tower Building   80 Maiden Lane
11 York Road   Suite 704
London   New York
SE1 7NX   NY 10038

British Library Cataloguing-in-Publication Data
A catalogue record for this book is available from the British Library.

ISBN: 0-8264-9024-7 (paperback)

Typeset by Servis Filmsetting Ltd, Manchester
Printed and bound in Great Britain by Biddles Ltd, King's Lynn,
Norfolk

Contents

Acknowledgements

This book is a culmination of many experiences over the last 20 years.

As a science teacher I had no idea that my Science degree would lead to an interest not so much in the individual subject matter of Biology and Chemistry, but in the Biology and the Chemistry of the individuals that I was teaching in the classroom.

This book is based on a number of observations made during the experiences of teaching children and management of teachers in London and Newcastle on Tyne in the UK and Washington in the USA. It is basically a record of the students and colleagues that I met on this journey.

Special thanks go to Dr Andy Briers, who is the inspiration of the Safer Schools Partnership programme in UK schools, and to his colleagues Paul Dunn whose work on the Acceptable Behaviour Contract has quite simply but not easily changed many people's lives for the better.

In addition Chris and Phil Smart of Special Needs Information Press (www.snip-newsletter.co.uk) have been major influences regarding many issues discussed throughout this book. In my opinion they have for some years produced the best resource for SEN that I have come across. I am indebted to them for their support and advice.

I would also like to pay tribute to Alexandra and Christina at Continuum for their encouragement, patience and expert advice in the production of this project.

Finally, last and not least my mother-in-law Nancy Wenzler, whose words 'publish or perish' provided the momentum to get many of these thoughts into print.

Believe the best in people and keep the faith.

Fin O'Regan
13.08.06

Preface

There is a great deal of controversy surrounding the issue of poor and inappropriate behaviour in schools today. Much of the debate centres on the question of whether this is a result of a range of developmental issues within a child's make-up, or whether it is a combination of sociological, environmental, or even changes in spiritual values, that exist in our society today.

Whatever the origins and causes, and we will touch upon some of these later on, the fact remains that teachers are increasingly having to manage a huge range of behaviours, including some children who are not just 'naughty' but demanding, disruptive, deceitful and even destructive.

These are the children for whom when the register is called and they are absent (and of course they seldom are) you, the teacher, and possibly some of the other students, breathe a sigh of relief!

This book attempts to unpick the key issues relating to inappropriate behaviour observed in schools today. Due to the fact that there has been so much discussion about challenging behaviour, it has been impossible for me to cover all areas. For example, I have made no attempt in this book to cover the issue of exclusion. What I have done however, is to offer a range of suggestions, strategies and schemes to deal with some forms of Behavioural, Emotional and Social Difficulties.

Written from the perspective of an experienced headteacher who has taught for over 18 years in both mainstream and special schools, not to mention having been an LEA SEN Advisor, governor of a primary school and a parent of three young children, my main objective is to provide a practical and pragmatic approach to the issue of behaviour management for all teachers, trainees and support staff.

Overview

The first chapter of this book attempts to define what challenging behaviour actually is. It provides an overview of the key risk factors that some individuals face as well as how their situation is influenced by their own family and the wider community. I touch on the nature versus nurture debate, including genetic issues, as well as the major factors affecting boys and girls, and also the media's perception of child and adolescent issues.

Chapter 2 offers an overview of Attention Deficit Hyperactivity Disorder (ADHD). I explain why this medical term is often driven by nature, and why it is a 'can't learn' issue and as a result needs a multifaceted approach, including school intervention, behaviour modification and sometimes medical options.

Chapter 3 provides an overview of Oppositional Defiant Disorder (ODD). It shows how children with this particular disorder have a tendency to 'get in your face'. I show how the 'won't back down' approach works best, and touch upon some other options for teaching and managing such students.

Chapter 4 provides a review of the key issues arising from students with Conduct Disorder. These children display a much greater range of challenging behaviour and can be some of the most difficult to manage.

In Chapter 5 you will find a definitive approach to Behaviour Management, the SF3R Model. Although it sounds complicated, 'S' stands for the 'Structure' or the 'Systems' for behaviour management, which is backed up by 'flexibility' to maintain those systems. Structure provides safety and security, though to support and sustain those systems the three Rs of 'Respect', 'Relationships' and 'Role' models will be required.

In Chapter 6 I introduce the idea of BACs – Behaviour Action Contracts. These are contracts drawn up between the school and the parent or parents. I then deal with the idea of proposed reinforcement options by parents, as well as outlining the role of the Peer Mentor.

Chapter 7 looks at two key features of challenging behaviour, namely bullying and anger management.

Chapter 8 outlines the key elements of the Safer Schools Partnership and introduces the option of ABCs (Acceptable Behaviour Contracts).

Chapter 9 provides an array of some of the alternative treatment options available for the management of behaviour, including the medication choices available for ADHD and ODD. It also looks at the issue of food, in particular the impact of diet, as well as some alternative ways of treating individuals.

Chapter 10 considers the key issue of depression, and how both counselling and coaching can help children with behavioural issues.

Chapter 11 looks in detail at the role parents play in working with schools in the context of behaviour management. It also takes a brief look at the Steer Learning report.

Chapter 12 looks at how many young people can live very effective lives mainly through their own resilience, but also because of a number of key influential factors. It also look at the carers, and how they can stay fresh and effective, not always an easy task!

I end with a number of Case Studies. Here we consider range of student behaviour profiles and look at both short and long-term options for managing their behaviour.

1 What Do We Mean by Challenging Behaviours?

The term 'behaviour', according to the dictionary, is to 'act or function in a particular way'. Meanwhile the word 'challenging' is defined as being 'difficult and stimulating'. So, in a nutshell this defines the role of the modern teacher in the inclusive classroom; namely, a manger of a group of 'difficult but stimulating "creatures" all acting in a particular way'.

During the course of this book we will be dealing specifically with how to manage some of the most common areas of discipline in schools today and, to some extent even more importantly, how to prevent the problems from occurring in the first place.

When we talk of children who exhibit persistent challenging behaviours we are talking about specific individuals for whom the regular rules of engagement (i.e. praise and consequences) do not work with any degree of consistency. These are the children who, when they have behaved inappropriately and are being verbally told off by a frustrated and possibly angry teacher, react in the following way instead of looking suitably apologetic:

- Say 'Sorry, Miss' but carry on doing it two minutes later.
- Ignore you . . . or perhaps even . . .
- Smile at you.

Teaching and behaviour management go hand in hand and are key elements of the job of any teacher, regardless of age group.

Recently a task force for behaviour has been created within the UK headed by Sir Alan Steer (the details of which appear in Chapter 11) to tackle what is being seen as an epidemic. Indeed, figures published by the Department for Education and Skills (DfES) suggest we do appear to have more of a problem with special educational

Table 1.1 Percentage of pupils with SEN in compulsory education: a global perspective (DfEs Statistics, January 2004)

	Per cent
UK	18.17
USA	11.17
Spain	4.27
Belgium	4.86
Germany	4.01
Japan	1.06

Table 1.2 Percentage of SEN pupils with emotional and behavioural difficulties or autism: a global perspective (DfEs Statistics, January 2004)

	Per cent
UK	26.86
USA	8.95
Spain	3.28
Belgium	5.3
Germany	7.48
Japan	15.09

needs (SEN) and, in particular, behaviour, when comparison is made with some other countries. As you can see from Table 1.1, we in the UK are much more likely to find SEN in mainstream education than even the USA, while in Japan it appears that SEN is either not found or a different set of criteria has been applied.

What's more, Table 1.2 shows that almost 27 per cent of SEN students in the UK had issues mainly relating to behaviour.

As a result of the figures in Tables 1.1 and 1.2 we find that almost 5 per cent of all children in UK schools are regarded as having emotional and behavioural difficulties or autism, that is the equivalent of 1.5 students in every class (that is of course, if one can have 0.5 of a pupil).

The other issue of course is that the term EBD or Emotional Behavioural Difficulties no longer exists and has been replaced by the term Behavioural, Emotional and Social Difficulties (BESD). This in itself makes the observation that society is a major factor in challenging behaviour, a point we will be addressing further in a later chapter.

Behaviour History

Since we appear so fond these days of saying that behaviour is worse than it used to be, it may be useful to look at some key articles written about behaviour in the 1970s.

In looking at the key factors that make a school effective, Rutter (1979) in *Fifteen Thousand Hours* and Reynolds in *The Process of Schooling* (1976) found that the ethos of a school is a composite number of factors but, more importantly, that these combined factors had a significant effect upon behaviour and the way in which pupils learn. The key findings were:

1 The school had a common policy on pupil behaviour which meant that they had generated consistent approaches among staff. This in turn had minimized erratic, unfair and idiosyncratic systems.
2 Regular use was made of rewards, ranging from praise for good work to a system of rewards throughout the school.
3 Pleasant working conditions were promoted throughout the school – work was displayed on the walls, classrooms were well decorated, and teachers brought in plants from home.
4 Effective use was made of classroom management techniques.
5 Emphasis was placed upon the importance of a close parent–school relationship.

So there you have it . . . the answer for behaviour management lay all the time in Homebase . . . with a couple of good pot plants you can achieve anything . . .!

Many other studies in both the UK and US, including the Elton Report (1989), which conducted a massive survey on behaviour in school and made no fewer than 138 recommendations, have basically found eight common themes on which they agree. They feel the following help to minimize the effectiveness of behaviour management:

1 Leadership role of the headteacher
2 Teacher involvement
3 Pupil involvement

4   Parental involvement
5   Curriculum organization
6   Use of a Positive Discipline Plan
7   Use of effective management strategies
8   Use of effective programmes for managing individual learning and behavioural needs.

The essential tool of applying good behaviour in a school will be determined by the Behaviour Policy, in which both the philosophy and the basic principles of Rules, Rights and Responsibilities should be outlined in order to create a caring community atmosphere in all schools.

Behaviour and Inclusion

The policy of inclusion in mainstream schools has created a wider range of challenges to teachers in terms of learning and behaviour and has been supplemented by many additional policies to support this process. These include the revised SENDA Act (2001) and the recent publication *Removing Barriers to Achievement* (DfES, February 2004) which in itself complements the proposals identified in the Green Paper 'Every Child Matters' and sets out the Government's vision in improving provision for children with SEN in four key areas:

- early interventions
- removing barriers to learning
- raising expectations/achievement
- delivering improvements in partnerships.

Although of course not all children with SEN will exhibit behavioural difficulties, as well as children with behavioural difficulties not necessarily having SEN, the correlation between the two groups remains strong. The document emphasizes the fact that all teachers should expect to teach children with SEN and that all schools should play their part in educating children from their local community regardless of their background or ability.

The National Association of Special Educational Needs (NASEN) defined inclusion, in 2000, in the following terms:

- Every human being has an entitlement to personal, social and intellectual development and must be given an opportunity to achieve his or her potential in learning.
- Every human being is unique in terms of characteristics, interests, abilities, motivation and learning needs.
- Educational systems should be designed to take into account these wide diversities.
- Those with exceptional learning needs and/or disabilities should have access to high quality and appropriate education.

Meanwhile the key elements of providing for inclusive education include:

- Purposeful and sensitive leadership/school ethos
- Academic standards
- Curriculum content
- Quality of teaching
- Quality of resources
- Access to latest research
- In-service training
- Attitudes of staff
- Teacher self-esteem
- Multi-agency cooperation
- School–community links
- Home–school links
- Pupil attitudes to school
- Pupil self-esteem
- Standards of attendance and behaviour
- Interpersonal relationships.

Understanding Behaviour

In dealing with behaviour, some common themes or threads will occur. These include early intervention, developing relationships and the option of multi-agency intervention. We will explore the practical applications of these issues in the main part of this book.

As a teacher dealing with behaviour issues, there will be certain issues that you will be able to deal better with than others. It can be most helpful to assess your own skills in dealing with those that you do well and those that you may have some problems with.

Inappropriate behaviours can be classified into three specific areas in terms of their impact on the individual, their peers and the overall situation:

Overall behaviours

Demanding	Bossy, volatile, argumentative
Destructive	Disruptive
Physically and verbally abusive/aggressive	Accident prone
	Distractible
Interferes with others	Immorality
Lack of self-control	Lies
Restless/fidgety	Steals
Talks all the time, talks back to staff	Phobias

Learning behaviours

Cannot get started	Easily distracted
Underachieves	Procrastinates
Works too slowly/ quickly	Poor motivation, easily frustrated
Forgets instructions/ explanations	Difficulty in completing tasks
Off task, lazy	Avoidance
	Disorganized

Socialization behaviours

Anxious	Low self-esteem
Selfish	Loud/quiet
Egocentric	Boisterous
Rude	Thoughtless
Insensitive	Withdrawn

| Immature | Without feeling/empathy |
| Depressed | Doesn't take turns |

Being specific about the key behaviours that are having the greatest impact in preventing the learning process for a specific child or a group of children is the key point in behaviour management. With certain pupils, who may exhibit a range of difficult behaviours, it can sometimes seem impossible to find a starting point, but in order to affect change the range of behaviours needs to be broken down one by one. This is why it is often useful to classify behaviours into those which have had the greatest impact, rather than the more minor ones such as fidgeting, which although might be annoying is hardly a 'crime against the state'.

Being able to specifically deal with the most serious types of behaviour will help teachers to understand which strategies and solutions can be developed to modify the impact.

Having said this, the basis of successful behaviour management systems for children is for the teacher to 'set out their stall' by providing clear and consistent behavioural expectations for all individuals within the group.

Reasons for Behaviour Problems

The reasons for challenging behaviour are as wide and complex as the behaviours themselves. Responsible factors can be developmental or sociological, and are often a combination of both. The issue regarding parents who do not, or seem unable to, set boundaries or rules at home can play a significant part in poor behaviour being transferred into the school; however it does appear that in many cases it is specifically developmental issues or difficulties with the child as opposed to the external environment that play the major part in challenging behaviours in the classroom.

There are a range of developmental labels, such as Attention Deficit Disorder, Autistic Spectrum Disorder, Conduct Disorder, Emotional and Behavioural Difficulties, and Oppositional Defiant Disorder, to name but a few. These specific issues have a range of diagnostic criteria, which seldom occur in isolation and often overlap alongside specific learning difficulties such as dyslexia and dyspraxia.

The other issue to consider is that we now believe many developmental issues may be genetically linked within the family gene pool. Therefore we could also have the situation of a 'double whammy effect' of a developmentally dysfunctional child from a home with one or more developmentally dysfunctional family members. It could therefore be said these parents 'can't' as opposed to 'won't' set traditional rules, boundaries or expectations because they really don't know how to this in a more traditional way.

As a result early identification of any potential developmental issues is the key to long-term success and therefore teachers need to trust their instincts in terms of early identification of which individuals 'are at risk'. Too often the call of 'he will grow out of it' or 'he is just tired' is given to explain away what is perceived as inappropriate behaviour. While individual children will all have individual personalities and will present different responses to certain situations, the role of the teacher is not just to teach children subject matter but to help them to manage and adapt to different situations. They need to individualize their approach.

It may be helpful to conduct an initial 'risk assessment' for children who may well exhibit difficult behaviour in the school environment. Some of the factors to look out for are listed below.

Risk factors in the child themselves

- Specific learning difficulties
- Communication difficulties
- Specific developmental delay
- Genetic influence
- Difficult temperament
- Physical illness, especially if chronic and/or neurological
- Academic failure
- Low self-esteem.

Risk factors in the family and community

- Overt parental conflict
- Family breakdown
- Inconsistent or unclear discipline
- Hostile or rejecting relationships
- Failure to adapt to a child's changing needs
- Physical, sexual or emotional abuse
- Parental criminality, alcoholism or personality disorder
- Death and loss – including loss of friendship
- Socio-economic disadvantage
- Homelessness
- Disaster
- Discrimination
- Other significant life events.

Although the above lists are not exhaustive, they does provide a starting point in identifying certain factors that might contribute towards potential difficulties. That said, we must be careful that child or family reputations are not forged on the basis of an older sibling who may have had behavioural problems at the school or be well known within the surrounding community.

Behaviour in Context

The key element of a Behavioural Risk Assessment is that being 'proactive' rather then 'reactive' in planning for behaviour management/modification may be a worthwhile investment for the future.

The label BESD currently covers a continuum of severity and the full range of ability. It describes pupils whose difficulties present a barrier to learning and persist despite an effective school behaviour policy and curriculum.

At the milder end of the BESD continuum pupils have difficulties with social interaction and find it hard to work in a group or cope in unstructured time. They may have poor concentration, temper outbursts and be verbally/physically aggressive to peers. Some children may display signs of low self-esteem, underachievement and inappropriate social interaction, but do not have behavioural outbursts. They may also be withdrawn, quiet and difficult to communicate with. Other children provoke peers and are confrontational or openly defiant and sometimes physically aggressive towards adults. They have a short attention span. Their self-esteem is low and they find it hard or impossible to accept praise or take responsibility for their behaviour. Some children cannot function in groups at all and exhibit persistent and frequent violent behaviour, which requires physical restraint.

Boys and Behaviour

It does appear that, regarding behaviour, 'boys make all the noise'; indeed, it is a fact that boys are 12 times more likely to shout out in class than girls and at least four to five times more likely to have learning/behavioural difficulties.

Why is this? Well, part of the answer lies in difference in brain function. Steve Biddulph in his book *Raising Boys* (1997) makes the well-researched point that in all children the left cortex of cortex of the brain grows more slowly than in the right, but that in boys this is delayed further. As boys develop more reconnections are made on the right side, making them richer in internal connections, whereas girls achieve a greater degree of cross-connection between the hemispheres. It is for this reason that girls who may have learning problems improve more quickly than boys. This situation is also supported by the fact that boys are more prone to brain damage at birth. They are also far more likely to suffer from autism, ADHD, dyslexia, dyspraxia, etc.

Although it is dangerous to provide a simple generalization, it does appear that because girls have better inter-neural links between both hemispheres in the brain they are better equipped to handle issues that need both sides working in harmony. This would include skills such as reading, writing and emotional and reflective abilities. Boys, in contrast, appear more geared to activities governed by the right side of the brain, such as practical and mathematical skills.

It is important to make the point that practice in all of the above skills help to make permanent connections through teaching, etc., and that these differences are both slight, do not apply to all individuals, and, most importantly, do not have to be accepted as limitations.

In terms of behavioural differences between the sexes it is important to make the point that certain characteristics do not refer to all boys or all girls but that certain trends or traits are often seen (or least appear to demand greater attention).

Greg Griffiths, in his book *Managing Boys' Behaviour* (2002), compares Girl and Boy Traits:

Girls tend to	*Boys tend to*
Move quietly in corridors	Move physically and loudly
Bring equipment	Do not bring equipment
Complete homework	Do not complete homework
Focus on quality work	Focus on completing tasks
Ask fewer questions	Want to ask more questions
Ask questions appropriately	Want an immediate response
Watch during practical sessions	Dominate during practicals
Not participate when engaged	Disrupt when not engaged
Discuss work	Work alone
Discuss personal issues	Discuss sport or movies
Cooperate with others	Compete with others
Comply more readily	Test instruction
Be able to ignore disruption	Move off task more readily
Accept redirection	Confront redirection

In many ways however, dealing with challenging behaviours and with those children who exhibit it, is as much a matter of how you the teacher perceive the situation as how you handle it. If challenging behaviour is seen as a problem then it will be a problem; if it is seen as a challenge, or indeed as an opportunity, it will be akin to taking a journey that, yes, will be frustrating and stressful, but also stimulating and fun.

Overall, the proactive, rather than the reactive, behaviour management approach will prevent many situations and incidents developing and this will create an environment for productive and successful learning outcomes for most of the children concerned. This is certainly the case within the current inclusive environment, as this will often provide challenges that necessitate additional support and resources in order to complement the pupil's existing provision. Some children will be learning how to learn and how to behave in the company of others who are following more traditional styles.

This multi-agency approach should not be seen as failure on the individual teacher's part; rather, a realization that some issues are more complex and that support is required in addition to good behaviour management principles. There is no doubt, however, that the spectrum of behaviour is vast and the term BESD, though useful, needs to be more specific in order to understand the different styles of challenge that teachers face.

In the next three chapters I attempt to break down BESD into three specific categories: Attention Deficit Disorder (can't learn but want to), Oppositional Defiant Disorder (won't learn but might) and Conduct Disorder (don't care).

By looking at these issues perhaps we can try to develop a plan of action for different individuals who present us with different challenges message. Although often in practice all three overlap in specific individuals, we might suggest that to some extent ADHD represents the behaviour in BESD, ODD the emotional and CD the social factors.

Let's see if you agree!

2 Can't Learn – Attention Deficit Hyperactivity Disorder

Attention Deficit Hyperactivity Disorder (ADHD) is so often regarded as purely a behavioural issue but it is often clearly misunderstood. The individuals will often be regarded as deliberately acting out and being distractible, disruptive and defiant. In fact in most cases those affected do not set out to be hyperactive, inattentive or impulsive but have problems in self regulation or control of certain aspects of their behaviour in much the same way that individuals who have autism or even Tourette's Syndrome do. Both conditions, by the way, often overlap ADHD.

ADHD children start off in the 'Can't learn but want to' category but as they get older and become somewhat battered and bruised by the external responses from parents, teachers and peers may move quickly into a 'Won't learn' or 'Don't care' state.

Somewhat ironically, when one considers the symptoms of ADHD and the professor's surname, the first person reputed to have identified the condition in the UK was Professor George Still (in 1902). Professor Still conducted a study of a group of children who showed an 'abnormal incapacity for sustained attention, restlessness and fidgetiness'. He reasoned that the children had serious deficiencies in 'volitional inhibition' of a biological origin, or something from within the child was responsible for the behaviour. Until then, students or pupils who exhibited features of impulsivity, hyperactivity or inattention were thought of as being simply the product of poor parenting or poor diet – in some ways, in over a hundred years some opinions have remained constant!

Still's theory of the disorder being caused by factions 'within' the child and not environmental reasons received further support from Bradley (1937). He made a chance discovery that the psychostimulant amphetamine could reduce levels of hyperactivity and behavioural problems. As a result the terms Minimal Brain Damage/Dysfunction were used until the late 1950s. At this point the emphasis shifted from an internal biological description to a behavioural expression, as hyperactivity became the defining feature.

This system of analysing the 'symptoms' as a means of explaining the 'syndrome' was further advanced by the conviction held by a number of influential researchers that attention rather than hyperactivity was the key. As a result 'attention' became the key word and since then there have been repeated attempts at reformulation, leading to the current classification in the Fourth Edition of the American Psychiatric Association (DSM IV) in 1994, the details of which have been adapted for this book and are listed below.

ADHD: Predominately Inattentive Type

A Six (or more) of the symptoms listed below will have occurred for at least six months in two or more places, i.e. school and home, and appear inconsistent with those of their peers.

Inattention

(a) Often fails to give close attention to detail or makes careless mistakes in written work or other activities.

(b) Often has difficulty in sustaining attention in tasks or play.

(c) Often does not seem to listen when spoken to.

(d) Often does not follow through on instructions and fails to finish schoolwork, chores or duties in the workplace.

(e) Often have difficulty organizing tasks and activities.

(f) Often loses things necessary for tasks and activities.

(g) Often avoids, dislikes or is reluctant to engage in tasks that require sustained mental effort.

(h) Is often easily distracted.

(i) Is often forgetful in daily activities.

ADHD: Hyperactive Impulsive Type

B Six (or more) of the symptoms listed below will have occurred for at least six months in two or more places, i.e. school and home, and appear inconsistent with those of their peers.

Hyperactivity
(a) Often fidgets with hands or feet or squirms in seat.
(b) Often leaves seat in classroom.
(c) Often runs about or climbs excessively.
(d) Often has difficulty in playing or engaging in leisure activities quietly.
(e) Is often 'on the go'.
(f) Often talks excessively.

Impulsiveness
(g) Often blurts out answers before questions have been completed.
(h) Often has difficulty waiting turn.
(i) Often interrupts or intrudes on others.

ADHD: Combined Type: If six or more symptoms are displayed in both A and B.

Adapted from DSM 1V (1994)

The current status recognizes three types of ADHD.

The most severe form of ADHD is called 'Combined Type ADHD'. It depends on the presence to a significant degree of six of the nine criteria for attention plus six of the nine criteria for Hyperactivity–Impulsivity. In addition there must be evidence that the symptoms presented themselves before the age of seven years, that symptoms are manifested in at least two different settings, result in significant impairment of academic, occupational, social settings and cannot be better explained by another psychological or psychiatric condition.

The second type is called ADHD Inattentive Type, which requires at least six out the nine symptoms for Inattention and recognizes that certain individuals may have profound inattentiveness without impulsivity/hyperactivity. This is one of the reasons why in some textbooks you may find the ADHD term written with a slash as in AD/HD, in order to distinguish Inattentive ADHD with the third type known as Hyperactive Impulsive Type, which requires at least six out of the nine symptoms listed in the Hyperactive/Impulsivity section.

As a rule ADHD Inattentive Type refers to children who have greater difficulty with memory and perceptual motor speed, are prone to day-dreaming and often socially withdrawn. This is in contrast to Hyperactive/Impulsive Type.

Redefining ADHD

Professor Russell Barkley, the eminent world ADHD expert, argues that the key element of the ADHD condition is an inability to inhibit behaviours. In other words, people with ADHD are drawn to the present, there really is no future or past, just the 'now'. This is well illustrated in the following example clearly explained by Stan Goldberg (2005) in his excellent book *Ready to Learn*:

> When you step on a dog's tail it howls . . . no discussion occurs within the dog's brain . . . it is an instinctive reaction, a reflex . . . no inhibition takes place. Though no single part of the brain is involved with modulating behaviour it does appear the main areas for doing this are in our frontal and pre-frontal lobes. These frontal lobes consider where we came from and where we want to go and how to control ourselves about how we want to get there. This ability to put on the brakes allows us the luxury of thinking before we speak or act.

Goldberg argues that this lack of control or inability to apply the brakes is a central point for many of issues for the individual with ADHD and includes the following:

- Self talk
- Working memory
- Foresight (planning for the future)
- Sense of time
- Shifting agenda
- Separating emotion from fact.

How Common is ADHD?

Studies from ADDISS (Attention Deficit Disorder Information Services: The UK national ADD agency) in 2002 indicates that

5 per cent of the school–aged population are affected to some degree by ADHD, of which approximately 1 per cent are severely hyperactive. In addition 30 to 40 per cent of all children referred for professional help because of behaviour problems come with a presenting complaint associated with ADHD.

While more boys appear to be affected than girls, the ratio of boys to girls is considered to be somewhere in the region of 4:1 in both Combined and the Hyperactive Impulsive Types. Why this should be the case is open to much interpretation. What is clear is that boys and girls present the features of ADHD differently and to some extent parents and other adult supervisors treat them differently. The interesting fact, however, is that the ratio of boys to girls is seen to be 1:1 in the Inattentive Type category.

ADHD, Age and Intelligence

There is no age limit for children with ADHD although it is often difficult to diagnose in very young children. The effects will be extremely demanding and often difficult for both the individual and their family. These will be the children who stop getting invites to birthday parties of their peers as their behaviour may be unpredictable and even dangerous.

As children grow into teenagers many additional entrenched difficulties can arise after many years of struggling and failure at school. At this stage often the hyperactivity noted when younger is reduced; however, impulsivity, poor attentional skills and oppositional behaviour become more apparent. Adult ADHD is also a very real and often disabling condition and can result in a host of factors relating to employment and success in relationships with other people.

Though ADHD is found at every IQ level, most of the individuals may be of average or above average intelligence and ADHD may well mask intelligence in gifted children. Alternatively, high intelligence apparently enables children to cope academically, until some crisis point is reached, often during adolescence.

With a comprehensive approach to management, however, even those with severe ADHD can usually be effectively helped.

Impact of ADHD

A 1987 Report to the US Congress prepared by the Interagency Committee of Learning Disabilities attributes the probable cause of ADHD to 'abnormalities in neurological function, in particular to disturbance in brain neurochemistry involving a neurological class of neurotransmitters'. Researchers are unclear, however, as to the specific mechanisms by which these neurotransmitter chemicals influence attention, impulse control and activity level.

Although many ADHD children tend to develop secondary emotional problems, ADHD itself may be related to biological factors and is not primarily an emotional disorder. Nevertheless emotional and behavioural problems can frequently be seen in ADHD children due to problems that these children tend to have within their school, home and social environment. Such characteristics as inattentiveness, impulsivity and underachievement can also be found in non-ADHD students who suffer primarily from emotional difficulties, which effect concentration and effort. These students may have 'motivational' deficits leading to diminished classroom attentiveness and performance.

An important quote by the American writer Michael Gordon sums up the fundamental issues of ADHD:

> *The core deficit that ADHD children experience is a thick barrier between themselves and life's consequences.*

The main problem regarding ADHD is that children who suffer from it are mistaken for being uncooperative or plain naughty and do not respond to redirection in the same ways as traditional children. These can be the children who, when being told off by an adult, smile . . . not always an intended response but nevertheless highly annoying for the supervisor involved.

There is no doubt that early identification and intervention in teaching and managing students with ADHD can play a huge part in preventing secondary behavioural issues from developing.

In reality however, in every class of 30 children it is likely that there will be one or two students with ADHD. Due to the potential impact of these children on the class dynamics in terms of teacher time and social interaction, it could well be argued that ADHD either directly or indirectly affects every student in every classroom.

Although many teachers, support staff and administrators are aware of the term ADHD, few see it as medical disorder rather than a behavioural issue. This to some extent is understandable by the very fact that teachers at the 'chalkface' will have to address the core symptoms of inattention, impulsivity, hyperactivity and often other behavioural/socialization difficulties.

Generally, there is no doubt that parents in their dealings with the educational system regarding SEN generally, and ADHD in particular, often have very negative experiences, including lack of understanding by teachers, confusing and lengthy processes to obtain support through action plans, statementing, etc., and a lack of understanding by health care professionals. They often generally feel being in the dark and having to cope without support or information.

That ADHD has a significant impact on the lives of individuals themselves and their families is in no doubt, especially when we consider some of the effects of this condition, which we could list as follows:

- Lack of foresight/hindsight, i.e. always living for the moment
- Poor organizational skills, complete lack of time management
- Lack of social skills and reading social clues
- Poor frustration tolerance, being inflexible
- Risk taking/thrill-seeking behaviours
- Problems with transitions, problems paying attention to others
- Lying, swearing, stealing and blaming others.

For once, let's look at the perspective of parents. A mother wrote an article for the teachers at her son's school, which included pieces of advice for teaching staff:

Complaints about 'boredom' from the ADHD child, particularly about his class or schoolwork, should be noted. More often than not the real word the child is searching for is 'overwhelmed', though she may not make that jump. Your child actually may not be 'overwhelmed' with the work, the teacher, or even his classmates. Many times the feeling comes from something completely unrelated, which they are unable to work through and continue to process on. Consistency in daily activities helps with this a great deal, and allows the child the ability to refocus on what is front of him.

I know from experience with my son that his worry level is quite high at times. These 'times' can normally be related to just how often his daily routine has been altered. Life happens in our house. There have been family problems, financial problems, medical problems, the whole gambit; but what helps our children the most in these times is the daily routine. They can see these problems happening (ADHD children are quite observant during the most inconvient times), but study period still happened, and if study period still happened, then he doesn't worry as much. Life is going on, and he knows his place in the schema.

Many ADHD children think well while moving, or at the very least while standing. Work with this not against it. If you find your child works better standing then by all means set them up a higher desk area to work at. It is probably unrealistic to expect the school to do the same and probably not even a good idea (ADHD children have enough problems with feeling singled out). While at home however your child should be able to work in the most comfortable manner as possible. There have been many studies recently that show highly creative minds, such as graphic artists, also work better standing up. Therefore, this may not be strictly an ADHD phenomenon, and it is important to let our children know this as well.

Textures are so amazing with ADHD children. I find cottons are good clothing for my son, whereas polyesters or other unnatural fibres, and wools, are a constant source of distraction for him. However, textures can be helpful as well. I heard about a teacher who used Velcro strips taped to the underside of the school desks for her ADHD students so they could run their fingers across the rough surface. I tried this with my son's study desk and found it helped him concentrate while he read.

Smell can be a factor in refocusing. Lemon and strong peppermint seem to help. On the same topic I have found that crunching apples is good as well.

My friend's daughter is a 'tapper', she taps and drums constantly while reading. Telling her to 'sit still' or 'stop drumming' is right along the lines of 'stop breathing' for all the good it does. My friend solved this by getting a stress ball to work in her hands while she reads.

ADHD children are notorious for not being adept at figuring out how long a task will take to accomplish. They look at an assignment such as reading a short book and making a report about it as something that can be blown out in a single night. The trouble is they have some experience that backs this up for them. For instance, my son can read his fantasy novels at an amazing rate. Of course, it is not the same as the novella he is assigned to read, and he is not making reports about them either . . . two large factors that do not find their way into his own time-estimate equations.

ADHD and How It Overlaps with Other Conditions

Diagnosing ADHD requires awareness of the range of other co-morbid disorders associated with it (which may often accompany it), or in fact be mistaken for it. As a result, evidence and existence of these must be fully investigated before any clear diagnosis can take place:

- specific learning difficulties such as dyslexia
- dyspraxia and dyscalculia occur in 40 per cent of children with ADHD
- disruptive behavioral disorders such as Oppositional Defiant Disorder and Conduct Disorder occur in about 50 per cent of cases
- anxiety disorders occur in about 30 per cent of all ADHD individuals.

Impact of ADHD

Obviously co-morbid factors are not just associated statistics. The social and physiological implications can directly affect the life of the individual. In many cases individuals develop these other behavioural traits as they progress through life, especially when the initial problem is either misdiagnosed or overlooked.

One-way of assessing this is that to suggest the following pathway for an ADHD individual:

Age 7 – Key Stage 2	Low self-esteem

Age 11 – Key Stage 3	Disruptive behaviour, learning delay, poor social skills

Age 14 – Key Stage 4	ODD, challenging behaviour, criminal behaviour, school exclusion, substance abuse, Conduct Disorder, lack of motivation, Complex LD

Although there are many theories about social disintegration, lack of parental control, lack of discipline in schools, etc., a brief look at data collated by the Youth Justice Board in a 2003 report shows some interesting patterns:

- only 30 per cent of young offenders were with both of their parents
- 27 per cent had previous permanent exclusions
- 41 per cent were regularly truanting
- 42 per cent were rated as underachieving at school
- 40 per cent were assessed as associated with peers involved in criminal activity
- 25 per cent were assessed as having friends who were all offenders
- 50 per cent were recorded as having used cannabis
- 75 per cent were considered to be impulsive and to act without thinking
- 9 per cent were considered to be at risk of self-harm or suicide (15 per cent in the case of females).

Perhaps one way of looking at the situation is to take the view that students with ADHD are not so much 'attention seekers' but 'attention needers' and that teaching and management strategies must take on board a response to this unique learning style.

Managing ADHD

What therefore should be our approach? My firmly held view is that students with ADHD need the key components of *structure* and *flexibility*, which needs to be combined with the support of supervisors who are understanding and proactive.

There is no doubt that the issues change as children get older and move through the 'Can't learn' stage and into the 'Won't learn' and 'Don't care' phases. When younger, the children can be quite engaging, though 'full on' and disruptive.

A brief survey among children between the ages of 7 and 11 in a special school for children with ADHD and learning difficulties, conducted in London during March 2002, resulted in the following top tips for teachers about what it felt like to have the condition.

1 **Help me to concentrate and focus**: Generally I need to be touching and fiddling with something to help me to concentrate on what I am being asked to do. What can I use in order for me to stay on task that is not too annoying for the teacher?

2 **Don't sit me next to things or people who I know will distract me**: I cannot ignore other people sitting near me or things outside the windows. Also some things on the wall and ceilings make me want to look at them or play with them whenever I see them.

3 **I need to know what comes next**: I really like to know where I need to sit and what I am supposed to be doing and when I am working on something I really need some warning before I have to stop doing it.

4 **I need to know now, I really do:** Please let me know if I'm doing something right or wrong straight away. I really find it hard to wait my turn like some of the other kids. If I can't tell you can I have a different way of telling you like writing you a note or sending you a signal? Tap me on my shoulder if I am drifting off or looking around.

5 **I didn't forget, I never heard you**: I really find it hard to listen to lots of stuff. I sometimes hear the first one but not the

stuff after that, and then I forget the first one anyway. I need one instruction at a time.

6 **It's hard, I can't do it:** I get really frustrated very quickly when I can't do it and then I don't care anymore. Can you help me find a way of not giving up as easily as I really want to learn?

7 **Wait for me, I am still thinking, I am almost done now:** Can I have more time to do this work and how much do I get, can you remind me in 2 minutes? My memory is really bad. Is this ended, how much more is there to do?

8 **I didn't know I was doing it and I didn't know I said it**: Sometimes the first time I think about something it's too late. I have already done it or said it. Can you help me to Stop, Think and then Act.

9 **I can never find my pen:** I really can never find it, is there anyway you can help me with my materials as in can I leave them here with you and use them next time? If I take them with me I will lose them.

10 **It's too noisy for me, I need to go somewhere else**: Can you let me go and work somewhere else either in the room or outside it, the room sometimes is too busy for me?

11 **Why are you always shouting at me, it's not fair, you hate me don't you**: Please find me doing something good and tell me when I'm doing it! I know I do silly things and it is wrong of me and it's right to point these out but I don't do it to get at you. I really don't know why I do it

12 **It's wrong isn't it**: I'm really not very good at Maths and stuff, although I do get, sometimes get, things right most of my work has a lot of red pen in it.

Teenagers and ADHD

While all teenagers need supportive relationships, adolescents with ADHD are particularly in need of guidance from caring adults, especially when faced with academic and social adjustment problems. Teens who make it through tough times will need to do so in a supportive context. It appears to be a common factor that whether it was a particular teacher, counsellor or highly patient and proactive parent, the net result is always the same. The statement 'I had someone who cared' or 'someone believed in me' is so often the comment of the successful ADHD college student.

Relationships are the cornerstone of the action needed and are at least as important as the specific strategies employed. Strong emotional bonds between adults and teens provide the backdrop where failure and fears can be explored. This is where plans can be made about how to react in different problem situations, where motivation can be nurtured and encouragement given.

Medication and ADHD

Although medicating students for academic benefit is frowned upon by many educationalists, I have seen many students over the years benefit greatly from the positive effects of increased focus, attention and resultant self-esteem.

If you accept ADHD as a neurobiochemical condition caused by lack of specific neurotransmitters, then it is only common sense that a neurobiochemical solution is needed. It is thought that neurotransmitters are responsible for relaying information between/among various parts of the brain necessary for certain functions to take place (e.g. impulse control and concentration). Dysregulation in this complex chemical relay system can and would appear to cause emotional and behavioural problems. As stated by Paul Cooper in 1995, 'medication is employed not as a chemical cosh to sedate overactive or inattentive children but as a chemical facilitator that raises chronically low levels of activity in certain parts of the brain and so regulates the message carrying process' (Cooper and Ideus: *Chemical Cosh or Therapeutic Tool*, 1995).

The neuro-stimulants Methylphenidate (Ritalin) and Dexamphetaphine (Dexedrine) are the most commonly used and effective preparations for the treatment of ADHD. Dosage levels vary from individual to individual but the rule of thumb is 1.5 milligrams per kilogram of body weight for Ritalin and 0.75 milligrams per kilogram of body weight for Dexadrine over a four-hour activation period. On the whole students for whom medication is correctly prescribed are positive about its effects. Comments made by students include the following:

> *'When I'm on it [Ritalin], I work harder, and I'm nicer, but when I'm out of school [and not on Ritalin] I'm sometimes silly, or I act stupid, or do things that I wouldn't do.'*
>
> *'When I'm taking Ritalin I'm calmer. I can study more and when I'm not I really can't concentrate or anything.'*
>
> *'I can concentrate better on Ritalin. I get on with my work more, and I don't talk so much.'*

It is not true however that all children enjoy taking medication even though it may be helping them academically, behaviourally and socially. Some students do not like to feel different and more focused and can also be embarrassed by taking medication when in the same context as their peers. In addition, a minority of students may suffer from minor side-effects such as stomach upsets, especially in the early stages.

The best way of handling these issues is for the child to meet with the supervising paediatrician or psychologist to review the situation, at which time the rational and reasons for why it is being used can be explained in age-appropriate terms. As always, a judgement of benefits versus the costs needs to be considered. In addition, any side-effects can usually be eradicated by minor changes in dosage, or the time the pills are administered. In terms of side-effects, I can honestly say I have seen few if any negative reactions over the years, apart from the occasional lack of appetite that Ritalin generates (I must state, however, that my experience is mostly with this particular medication).

The truth is that the main side-effect is the 'bad press' that medication has generated in recent years. It could be argued that both aspirin and penicillin, which benefit large numbers of people, have the potential to effect specific individuals negatively, sometimes fatally. In the last 50 years no evidence exists of any serious side-effects from the stimulants and therefore the whole issue should be seen in the correct context.

One crucial aspect to bear in mind is that for any child on medication it is the parents who are in charge . . . not the doctors, physiologists or teachers. Although the decision as to whether or not medication is prescribed is with the physician, the consumers of medical services have a choice as to whether they follow the professional's prescription or reject it. The client's right to choose is essential, but the validity of choice however depends on the foundations on which it rests.

Summary of Key Strategies for the Management of ADHD

1 Minimize distractions, maintain a clutter-free environment.
2 Seat proactively within the classroom environment.
3 Set realistic expectations in both task setting and time in specific assignments.
4 Create options for fidgeting, distraction, calling out, time keeping, and interaction.
5 Make additional provision for unstructured activities.
6 Consider medication for severe symptoms.
7 Develop close ties between home and school.

3 Won't Learn – Oppositional Defiant Disorder

Oppositional Defiant Disorder (ODD) is diagnosed when a child displays a certain pattern of behaviours that includes losing his or her temper frequently, defying adults, being easily annoyed and deliberately annoying others. These are the individuals not to get into an argument with. It is a less extreme behaviour than Conduct Disorder but, left untreated, can develop into some of the more antisocial behaviours associated with this condition.

Though full diagnostic criteria are listed in this chapter, the key elements are that these are children who display the following characteristics:

- argue with adults
- refuse and defie
- angry and defensive
- spiteful and vindictive.

In essence, they display a 'counter-will' against authority, especially when frustrated or stressed. They are often completely inflexible in these situations and the more pressure we apply to make them conform the greater the opposition.

The reasons and origins of this condition are difficult to specify but often the pattern will indicate frustration and intolerance as a result of some other type of special educational need. Examples include ADHD or dyslexia, lack of structure and patience in early child development, low academic, achievement, low self-worth, or a combination of some or all of these.

In many ways these are the 'Won't learn' category of child, likely to say 'you can't make me, it's not fair', '**** off' and 'whatever'.

The ODD pupil is likely to cause teachers and parents the most grey hairs and sleepless nights. These are students who need to look good in front of friends, be seen to win the argument, and have the last word.

Diagnostic Criteria for Oppositional Defiant Disorder

A pattern of hostile and defiant behaviour lasting at least six months, during which four or more of the following are present:

1   Often loses temper.
2   Often argues with adults.
3   Often actively defies or refuses to comply with adults' requests or rules.
4   Often deliberately annoys people.
5   Often blames others for his or her mistakes or behaviour.
6   Is often touchy or easily annoyed by others.
7   Is often angry or resentful.
8   Is often spiteful and vindictive.

Note: Consider a criterion met only if the behaviour occurs more frequently than is typically observed in individuals of comparable age and developmental level.

Adapted from DSM 1V (1994)

All of the criteria above include the word 'often'. But what exactly does this mean? Recent studies have shown that these behaviours occur to a varying degree in all children; however, researchers have found that the 'often' is best solved by use of the following criteria.

Has occurred at all during the last three months

- is spiteful and vindictive
- blames others for his or her mistakes or misbehaviour.

Occurs at least twice a week

- is touchy or easily annoyed by others
- loses temper
- argues with adults
- actively defies or refuses to comply with adults' requests or rules.

Occurs at least four times per week

- is angry and resentful
- deliberately annoys people.

No one knows for certain what causes ODD but the usual pattern is for problems to begin early in life, often before the age of five. Factors that will strongly influence the presence of ODD in the child will often be linked to issues of family dysfunction, including alcoholism and crime.

ODD is diagnosed in the same way as many other psychiatric disorders in children which involve a multimodal diagnosis, including a review of the medical history.

Over 5 per cent of children have ODD and although in younger children it is more common in boys than girls, as they grow older the rate is the same in males and females.

It is exceptionally rare for a child just to have ODD, as usually there will be ADHD or Conduct Disorder as well. However, it is worth making the point that ODD is characterized by aggressiveness, but not impulsiveness. In ODD, kids annoy you purposefully, while it is usually not so purposeful in ADHD. ODD signs and symptoms are much more difficult to live with than ADHD, although children with ODD can sit still. An ADHD child may impulsively push someone too hard on a swing and knock the child down on the ground but afterwards she would likely be sorry she did this. A child with ODD plus ADHD might push the kid out of the swing and say she didn't do it.

It can sometimes be difficult to like children with ODD. The destructiveness and wishful disagreement are purposeful. They like to see you get mad. Every request can end up as a power struggle. Lying becomes a way of life, and getting a reaction out of others is the chief hobby. Perhaps hardest of all to bear, they rarely are truly sorry and often believe nothing is their fault. After a huge blow up, the child with ODD is often calm and collected. It is often the teacher who looks as if they are going to lose it, not the child, and this is understandable as probably they have just been tricked, bullied, lied to, or have witnessed temper tantrums which know no limits. Children and adolescents with ODD produce strong feelings in people. They spend their time trying to get a reaction out of people, and are often successful in doing so.

The following are some examples of how ODD looks across the ages.

Infant Marianne

Marianne is now four years old. Her parents were very excited when she turned four – they hoped that perhaps it would mean that the terrible twos were finally over. They were not. Marianne begins her day by getting up early and making noise. Her father unfortunately has mentioned how much this bothers him. So she turns on the TV, or if that has been mysteriously disconnected, bangs things around until her parents come out. Breakfast is the first battleground of the day. Marianne does not like what is being served once it is placed in front of her. She seems to be able to sense how hurried her parents are. When they are very rushed, she is more stubborn and might refuse it altogether. It would be a safe bet that she would tell her mother that the toast tastes like poo. This gets her the first 'time out' of the day.

In the mornings she goes to preschool or goes off with her grandmother or to her aunt's. Otherwise Marianne's mother is unable to do anything. Marianne cannot entertain herself for more than a few moments. She likes to spend her time purposefully annoying her mother, at least so it seems. Marianne plays with it about one minute and says, 'Let's do something'. Her mother reminds her that they are doing something, the very thing that Marianne has been demanding for the last hour. 'No, let's do something else.'

So after Marianne's mother screamed so hard she was hoarse when her husband came home, Marianne gets to go out almost every morning. At preschool she is almost perfect, but will not ever do exactly what the teacher wants. Only once has she had a tantrum there. Marianne gets along with the other children as long as she can tell them what to do.

What sets Marianne off is not getting to do what Marianne wants.

Primary School Ryan

Ryan is ten. Ryan's day usually starts out with arguing about what he can and cannot bring to school. His mother and his teacher have now made out a written list of what these things are. Ryan was bringing a calculator to school and telling his teacher that his mother said it was all right. At first his teacher wondered about this, but Ryan seemed so believable. Then Ryan brought a 'little [Ryan's words] knife'. That led to a real understanding between the teacher and Ryan's mother.

Ryan does not go to school on the bus. He gets teased and then retaliates immediately. Since it is impossible to supervise bus rides adequately, his parents and the school gave up and his mother usually drives him to school. It is still difficult to get him there on time. As the time to leave approaches, he gets slower and slower. Now it is not quite as bad because for every minute he is late he loses 10 pence from his daily allowance. Once at school, he usually gets into a little pushing with the other kids in those few minutes between being under his mother's eye and the teacher's. The class work does not go too badly. Between the daily allowances which are geared to rewarding good behaviour he manages all right. This is good for everyone. At the beginning of the school year he would flip desks, swear at the teacher, tear up his work and refuse to do most things.

Break time is still the hardest time of the day. Ryan tells everyone that he has lots of friends, but if you watch what goes on in the lunch room or on the playground, it is hard to figure out who they are. Some kids avoid him, but most would give him a chance if he wasn't so bossy. The playground supervisor tries to get him involved in a football game every day. He isn't bad at it, but he will not pass the ball, so no one really wants him on their team.

After school was the time that made his mum seriously consider foster care. The homework battle was horrible. He would refuse to do work for an hour, then complain, break pencils and irritate her. This dragged thirty minutes of work out to two hours. So now she hires a tutor. He doesn't try all of this on the tutor, at least so far. With no homework, he is easier to take. But he still wants to do something with her every minute. Each day he asks her to help him with a model or play a game at about 4.30. Each day she tells him she cannot right now as she is making dinner. Each day he screams out that she doesn't ever do anything with him, slams the door, and goes in the other room and usually turns the TV on very loud. Three times she tells him to turn it down. He doesn't and is sent to his room. After dinner Ryan's dad takes over and they play some games together and usually it goes fine for about an hour. Then it usually ends in screaming. So Ryan's grandmother had the bright idea of inviting them over for supper at about eight o'clock most nights. But what about days when there is no school? Ryan's parents try very hard not to think about that.

Secondary School Tasha
Tasha is 15. She is in Year 10 and from her marks you would say there is no big problem. She is passing everything, but her teachers always comment that she is capable of much more if she tried. If they gave marks for getting along with others, it would be a different story. Tasha's best friend is currently doing a six-month sentence for vandalism and shoplifting. Tasha and Sylvie have been friends, if you can call it that, since the autumn. Since Tasha has almost no other friends, she will do anything to be Sylvie's friend. At least that is what her parents think. Tasha thinks it is 'cool' that Sylvie is at the Youth Centre. One sign of this friendship was that Tasha almost always gave her lunch money to Sylvie. Why? Because Sylvie wanted it. Tasha thought that Sylvie was her friend, but everyone could see that Sylvie was just using her. What seemed saddest to Tasha's parents is that Tasha could not see this at all. But this was nothing new. She would make a friend, smother them with attention, and that would be the end of it. Or the

friend would not do exactly what Tasha wanted and there would be a big fight and it would be over. But mostly Tasha complained that everyone bugged her. What seemed to save Tasha was the nursing home. Somewhere along the way Tasha got involved working there. To hear the staff there talk about her, you would never guess it was the same girl. Helpful, kind, thoughtful – they couldn't say enough positive things about her. In fact her parents joked that maybe if they all moved to the nursing home it would stop the fighting at home. They figured it out when another teenager volunteered to help one of the same afternoons as Tasha. Unfortunately the 'other' Tasha came out. She was tattling, annoying, disrespectful and hard to get along with. Tasha could get along with any one, as long as they weren't her age, a teacher, or a relative!

Top Tips for the Management of ODD

So what do you do to manage these pupils? As no one tactic or a group of tactics is guaranteed to work, a combination of some of the following suggestions may allow everybody concerned to have an easier time.

- **Give the student the opportunity to have their say.** If they need to get it out of their system, allow them the opportunity to do so. Perhaps give them the option to leave the room when about to 'pop'. However if they explode in public when having not taken the opportunity to leave, then you are entitled to follow up with further consequences.
- **Offer them a choice of outcome.** Following on from the situation above, they must often be given such a choice otherwise they will feel concerned and the sap will rise further. They need to feel as if they have some power, and you as the supervisor will need to allow them to 'own their behaviour' and the choice about what to do with it.
- **Focus on the incident not the student, don't personalize.** Teachers should always try to concentrate on the particular issue and never give the impression that they don't like the student, particularly with the ODD child.

Relationship building and respect are the key principles in working with these students. Nothing else really works long-term.

- **Use the broken-record technique, don't get drawn into the smokescreen or secondary behaviour.** Masters of their dark arts, the ODD student will try to take you within some convoluted reason for the issue. Don't be led astray. Stay focused on the issue at hand, saying over and over again what you wish to be the outcome. Nag if that's what it takes. This technique works.

- **Refer to rights and responsibilities and 'regret' the sanction if non-compliance occurs.** Always make sure the student knows the issue is not personal but that the rules are being infringed or challenged and therefore it is the business of the school. It is not you and them – it's just the way things are in this particular place at this particular time. Also, it is a good idea to deliver the sanctions with a shrug and sigh and give the impression you have no choice – it is just the way that life is!

- **Attempt to divert the student's attention by using distracting techniques.** As students with ODD are also likely to have aspects of ADHD then this tactic can also work to diffuse situations as they can be easily distracted.

- **Possible use of humour in some situations.** If students are in a confrontational mood, humour can, and indeed often does, change the course of many potentially damaging situations.

- **Use of behaviour action contracts and other professionals if defiance, anger, frustration occurs.** Although we will talk about this later, obviously in many cases other elements must be put into place before behaviour can be influenced and modified so as to change in the longer term. These include contracts and using specific professionals trained in helping students with sustained and deep-seated anger, frustration and poor self-esteem.

Many of the above options are simply a matter of mood management; that is, reading the mood of the student and deciding what course of action to take, and when and where. Often, it is as much about timing, rather than anything else.

Teachers who try to be competitive with the ODD student are seldom successful, and those who try a 'I'm in charge and your not' approach also do not get very far.

The ODD student, though inflexible when stressed, needs flexible management more than anything else, along with the need to save face in front of their peers. The same could be said to an even greater extent about Conduct Disorder, which will be discussed in detail in the next chapter.

Summary of Key Strategies for the Management of ODD

- Give the student the opportunity to have their say.
- Offer them a choice of outcome.
- Focus on the incident, not the student – don't personalize.
- Use the broken-record technique; don't get drawn into the smokescreen/secondary behaviour.
- Refer to rights and responsibilities and 'regret' the sanction if non-compliance occurs.
- Attempt to divert the student's attention by using distracting techniques.
- Possible use of humour in some situations.
- Use of behaviour action contracts and other professionals if defiance, anger or frustration occurs.

4 Don't Care – Conduct Disorder

This type of behavioural difficulty is where children often bully and show aggression to others. They may destroy property, including their own. If the condition occurs before ten years of age then the prognosis for effective treatment is poorer than if the condition occurs after this age. The difference between children with Conduct Disorder (CD) and ADHD is mainly one of wilful intent. A child with CD is more likely to premeditate, carry it out and have an alibi for the situation. In contrast, the first time an ADHD child thinks about a situation it is often too late as they have already carried out the action.

The four key elements that describe Conduct Disorder are:

- aggression to people/animals
- destruction of property
- deceitfulness or theft
- serious violations of rules.

These four areas are not mutually exclusive and the full criteria are shown on the following pages. What are the causes of this? Are certain children born to be destructive and violent? Well, once again, little evidence exists to support this. Rather, we are once again talking about a myriad factors: but in my opinion one that often occurs is a lack of or inappropriate role models. Other risk factors include biological, physiological and sociological factors. The net result is often that the CD individual, in contrast with the ADHD individual who 'Can't do' and the ODD individual who 'Won't do' (but might), simply doesn't care about his or her impact on the feelings and lives of others.

At present, research shows that in many respects CD is a more severe form of ODD, and although severe ODD can lead to CD, milder ODD usually does not. The common thread that separates CD and ODD is safety. If a child has CD there are safety concerns. Sometimes it is the personal safety of others in the school, family or community. Sometimes it is the safety of the possessions of other people in the school, family or community. Often the safety of the child with CD is a great concern. Children with ODD are likely to be an annoyance, but not especially dangerous. Children with CD usually are dangerous.

It is very common to see children with CD plus another one or two other issues. By far the most common combination is CD plus ADHD; between 30 to 50 per cent of children with CD will also have ADHD. Another common combination is CD plus depression or anxiety; one quarter to one half of children with CD will have either an anxiety disorder or depression. CD disorder plus substance abuse is also very common. Also common are associations with learning disorders, bipolar disorder and Tourette's Syndrome.

Diagnostic Criteria for Conduct Disorder

A repetitive and persistent pattern of behaviour in which the basic rights of others or major age-appropriate societal norms or rules are violated, as manifested by the presence of three (or more) of the following criteria in the past 12 months:

Aggression to people and animals
1   Often bullies, threatens or intimidates others.
2   Often initiates physical fights.
3   Had used a weapon that can cause serious physical harm to others (e.g. a bat, brick, broken bottle, knife, gun).
4   Has been physically cruel to people.
5   Has been physically cruel to animals.
6   Has stolen while confronting a victim (e.g. mugging, purse snatching, extortion, armed robbery).
7   Has forced someone into sexual activity.

Destruction of property

8   Has deliberately engaged in fire setting with the intention of causing serious damage.

9   Has deliberately destroyed others' property (other than by fire setting).

Deceitfulness or theft

10   Has broken into someone else's house, building or car.

11   Often lies to obtain goods or favours or to avoid obligations (i.e. cons others).

12   Has stolen items of non-trivial value without confronting a victim (e.g. shoplifting, but without breaking and entering, forgery).

Serious violations of rules

13   Often stays out at night despite parental prohibitions, beginning before the age of 13 years.

14   Has run away from home overnight at least twice while living in parental or parental surrogate home (or once without returning for a lengthy period).

15   Is often truant from school, beginning before the age of 13 years.

Adapted from DSM IV (1994)

About 30 per cent of Conduct Disorder children continue with similar problems into adulthood. It is more common for males with CD to continue on into adulthood with these types of problems than for females. Females with CD more often end up having mood and anxiety disorders as adults. Substance abuse is very high. About 50 to 70 per cent of ten year olds with Conduct Disorder will be abusing substances four years later. Cigarette smoking is also very high. A recent study of girls with conduct disorder showed that they have much worse physical health. Girls with Conduct Disorder were almost six times more likely to abuse drugs or alcohol, eight times more likely to smoke cigarettes daily, almost twice as likely to have sexually transmitted diseases, had twice the number of sexual partners, and were three times as likely to become pregnant when compared to girls without Conduct Disorder.

Theft

One of the areas that often needs to be addressed with students with CD is the issue of stealing or theft. This is not to say that at one time or another most students will not steal. Indeed, stealing is a very common behaviour; in fact some child psychiatrists would allege that it is normal survival behaviour for a young child to take something which excites their interest. Older children, however, eventually realize that the behaviour is wrong, but some may be unable to resist the impulse to appropriate items that are both available and desirable. The immediate gain often outweighs the possible consequences.

However, in contrast with students who are impulsive and do not plan their actions, children with CD are more premeditated. This means that with regards to this action they are often successful in not being caught in the act.

When a child or teenager knowingly takes something that does not belong to them, schools often have high levels of concern. There may be a temptation to criminalize the behaviour but this is unlikely to be an appropriate reaction, particularly if the child is young. The reaction to taking items needs to be closely related to the age of the perpetrator – and action to address it needs to be aimed at putting things right rather than eliciting punishment. It will instead be important to spend time locating the reason for the stealing and then taking action to remove the obvious temptation.

The reasons behind stealing can be complex. Some pupils for instance may simply desperately want something and see no other way of achieving it. Sometimes a child may steal as a show of bravery to peers or to give presents and become more popular at school. They may steal in order to provide income. There may be a need for more attention or the buzz gained from stealing may be attractive, especially to the child who has few other ways of gaining self-esteem.

It is likely that children with Conduct Disorder who steal from school are likely to have already taken things that did not belong to them at home and/or from local shops. It is likely that this behaviour has not been noticed and it may be difficult to discuss these issues with parents. The school may feel that parents may be hostile to the suggestion that their child has taken things that do not belong to them and fear the involvement of other agencies such as Social Services and the Police. Parents of older children may have problems in exercising control or influence upon their child's behaviour. However this behaviour should always be challenged, as research on young offenders often indicates that stealing when young was a defining feature of later offending behaviour. For older children, stealing is likely to be only one aspect of other behaviour that may lead to later social exclusion. Gottfredson and Hirsch's (1990) research, for instance, indicated that children who steal also tend to smoke, use alcohol and play truant more often than children who don't steal. Therefore action to reduce all antisocial behaviour needs to be planned with external and community agencies in order to impact on theft.

More important perhaps than the issue of who is taking things that belong to others, is the question of what is being stolen.

- Is it food or drink?
- Is it classroom kit (pens/pencils/PE kit)?
- Is it money?
- Is it the latest fad?
- Is it fairly expensive and easy to sell items such as CDs and mobile phones?

Though independent action will need to take place for specific children, by far the best policy within the school environment is both to reduce the temptation and empower the other children to act as guardians of both their own and others' items. Some general points include:

- Having a clear policy, communicated to and agreed with parents, about unnecessary valuables being allowed on school premises.

- Removing as far as possible the need to bring money to school.
- Insisting on the clear marking of all possessions.
- Providing children with a secure place to store tuck and classroom materials.
- Ensuring that children are unable to enter unsupervised classrooms, cloakrooms, etc.
- Providing access to food and drink to discourage the need for pupils to take others' tuck/packed lunches, e.g. breakfast clubs.
- Providing a locked container for jewellery and other valuables.
- Encouraging parents to obtain insurance cover to redeem loss, particularly in the case of expensive items such as lap-tops.

All the above will need to be policed and rigorously implemented, so ways to complete this without causing conflict need to be discussed.

School assemblies and PHSE should regularly address the issue of the impact of taking things that belong to others, in order to encourage empathy. This might include ensuring that children know why stealing is wrong and how it affects those who have lost something. However, staff must ensure that the message conveyed is that it is the behaviour that is wrong and not the child.

Top Tips for the Management of Conduct Disorder

Management within the school community can be extremely difficult as many of the issues are and will be outside the teacher's remit. However, as with children with ODD and ADHD, children and adolecents with CD may not always be problematic in class. Having said that, many of the issues will not be far away from the surface and once again some basic tips on management are provided.

Try to read the mood of the student before choosing the strategy. As stated earlier so much of behaviour management is about reading the mood of a particular child and this is so true when it comes to dealing with children with CD.

Though these children often appear to have their own agenda it is still the case that certain situations will provide impetus for the flare up. With this in mind it may be useful to look at the analogy of how fires start. Fires of course need three main constituents to start – oxygen, a fuel, and a spark. If one of these can be removed then you have in essence doused the flames. Fires. . . .

- need oxygen: this is the mood or atmosphere in which emotions are occurring
- need a fuel: this is the mind reacting to the mood, causing thoughts/feelings such as fear or threat
- need a spark: this is the response to the mood, which is affected by a specific person or situation.

'Fires' are the body responding physically and verbally. As a result, if at any point in the process the mood can be changed, or the mind of the child is diverted elsewhere, or a specific person or situation removed, or the child's situation is adapted, then in theory you can put out the fire.

Identifying and assessing the mood is a skill but common signs of a potential flare up are:

- child unwilling to communicate
- child looking away when you speak
- pacing around, unwilling to remain in seat
- outbursts of temper
- frequent repeating of certain phrases
- rapid speech
- false, sarcastic laughter
- sweating, shortness of breath or rapid breathing
- unable to settle to work
- appears agitated
- eyes bulging/pupils dilated
- redness in the face
- muscles tense and fists clenched
- tightly closed lips
- stiff, rigid posture
- rapid body movements
- aggressive pointing figures
- enlarged space bubble created.

Some or all of the above should be assessed in your mood management analysis.

Finally, things *not to do*, because they are likely to fan the flames are:

- shouting
- not listening to their views
- bringing up past, unrelated misdemeanours
- standing toe to toe/face to face
- raising your voice in response to their's
- allowing conflict in a public forum
- other aggressive non-verbal communication – arms flailing, aggressive facial expressions.

Diffusing strategies or attempting to prevent the fires have largely been covered earlier in this book with regards to ODD and are appropriate here as well. However, the CD child is often more calculating and calmer than the ODD child and methods that include being calm but assertive when facing confrontations can also apply. In contrast with children with ODD, in these situations it is usually advisable not to appear too passive and to some extent be more assertive and match the mood of the situation.

Other key areas to consider in the management of students with CD are:

- the use of rewards and sanctions
- the use of contracts and multi-agency options
- looking for opportunities for the child to develop areas of interest, e.g. sport, music, these interests, such an interest produce a beneficial role model.

Though specific rewards and sanctions and even the types of contracts outlined in Chapter 6 can effect short period behaviour change, to some extent the individual may need a new direction or purpose in life so as to take them away from their 'Don't care' mentality. As a result, current role models who may be providing or sustaining negative attitudes might be replaced by other role models in order to affect real and lasting change. This is easier said than done.

Unfortunately, without such strategies and changes it will often be the case that children and adolescents with CD remain both challenging not just to school personnel but to the community as a whole.

Summary of Key Strategies for the Management of CD

- Try to read the mood of the child before choosing the strategy.
- Try to let the child save face in front of peers by providing a choice of options.
- Be calm and assertive when facing confrontations but do not appear too passive and do strive to match the mood of the situation.
- Be consistent with rewards and sanctions.
- Look for opportunities for the child to develop areas of interest, so as to allow influence of appropriate role models
- Look at the use of contracts and multi-agency options.

5 The Definitive Behaviour Management Model

During a speech by then Secretary of State for Education, Ruth Kelly, at a headteachers' conference in Blackpool in February 2005, she stated that 'Schools should take a zero-tolerance approach to classroom disruption' and that a focus was needed on 'low-level unruliness'. In addition, she suggested the use of 'off-site support systems to remove disruptive pupils from classrooms'.

We would all agree that teachers dealing with disruptive pupils need support, but clearly this approach makes a mockery of the policy of inclusion. In effect it highlights the long-held belief of teachers – flatly denied by LEAs and the government – that inclusion is fine for those children with specific learning or physical difficulties but is not an option in the case of a child still perceived to behave in a more demanding way.

So, as a result, what is the magic formula for success for these pupils? Do any answers really exists and can they be practically applied?

Of course there is no magic formula but it does occur to me that specific approaches, if combined together, can provide at least a framework for managing challenging behaviour.

The formula I propose is shown below.

Troubleshooting Challenging Behaviour = SF3R

SF3R? What do these letters and the number represent, where did this come about and what makes them seemingly work in harness together?

I am often asked on the lecture circuit what were the origins of this approach. Quite simply, it comes from observing good practice of colleagues who are successful in working with children with challenging behaviour.

In a previous role as an admissions officer in a secondary school I often found regarding children with behaviour issues that many clues about how to manage them lay in their past teacher reports from the primary school.

A lot of the reports would state that the child as a student is difficult, defiant, demanding, etc., the overall impression being that the individual teacher is frustrated, weary, often cross; basically, it appears from the written report that the teacher is not particularly fond of the specific child. However, within the pile of reports, often there is at least one report that is more positive and gives a very different impression about the child. When I ask the parent about this report and the teacher, a pattern usually emerges.

It often appears to be a female teacher and someone who had the child in either Year 3 or 4 during the primary school years. This teacher appeared to be very clear about her expectations regarding behaviour but tweaked aspects of her expectations with the child; for example he was allowed to stand up and write if he had problems sitting in his chair, or he often had jobs to do in and around the classroom. According to the parent he didn't always do 20 maths questions like the other kids; sometimes he did 10 and did a drawing. He didn't always go to the school assembly with the other kids but sometimes he and the LSA stayed in the classroom and put posters on the wall. During break times he often stayed in the classroom again and helped to feed and clean the hamster cage.

It sounded like someone was taking the temperature of the mood a lot of the time . . . was firm, fair and flexible and all sides knew what was expected of them. The other strange thing is that this teacher often appears to be 5 feet 2 inches and for some uncanny reason usually has a Scottish background.

This we can only refer to as the Miss Jean Brodie principle. The values of proactive behaviour management techniques seem bound up in combining a number of key principles used by effective school practioners, which can be summed up by five letters representing the five key words in SF3R, which are:

S = Structure – in essence the frameworks, systems, rules and regulations that all children need so badly.

f = Flexibility and how you can maintain those systems by applying some give and take over how elements of the structure are successfully adhered to.

The 3Rs on the other hand are those which will sell, support and sustain your systems and are as follows:

- Mutual 'Respect' is the starting point when working with non-traditional learners with behaviour issues. It may not happen overnight but it is up to us to offer the olive branch first, to even the most difficult student. We are the adults after all.
- 'Relationships' to foster academic and behavioural aims, objectives and an understanding of the differences within and between children.
- Positive 'Role' models to maintain academic and behavioural aims and objectives, i.e. someone else in the loop to sustain the momentum.

Some may argue that offering structure and flexibility working in harness is a contradiction, but in practice this in not the case. In reality they complement each other. In the course of this chapter I provide examples of how this works but another way of looking at this can be summed up in the following quote by Amos in 1997 when he said: 'Managing SEBD is about having "Rubber Boundaries"', i.e. structures, routines and systems for all which bend to meet and absorb individual needs but never break.

SF3R in Action

In some ways the analogy of the formula is not necessarily one that will work for everybody so instead we might want to think

Figure 5.1.   SF3R – cogs in the Behaviour Management machine

of each of these five terms as cogs in the Behaviour Management machine as shown in figure 5.1. We will now look at each of these areas in some detail and at how they operate together.

Structure
This encompasses many aspects of the organizational structures of the school and includes the following key areas, which we will look at in some detail:

1 Leadership and management
2 Teaching and learning targets
3 Behaviour expectations and application of rules
4 General classroom management

As mentioned in Chapter 1, overall success in behaviour management will be through *leadership and management* because without a focused and consistent approach students with challenging behaviour will often fall through in the cracks in the system.

1. Leadership and management
The area of leadership and management has a number of subsections:

- The personality, style and leadership of the headteacher, relationships between members of the senior management team (SMT), and communication within the teaching, care and support staff of the school.
- The selection, support and retention of staff in general.
- The clarity and consistent application of school policies.
- Monitoring and critical self-evaluation of the performance of the school and staff.

Quite simply, the leaders set the tone, and if improving challenging behaviour is really part of the agenda and the reasons and factors causing it are approached in a consistent, proactive, and not reactive way by the SMT, then the rest of the staff will pick up the ball. If cracks and/or major disagreements occur at this level the effect will filter down and that's where inconsistencies will occur.

Choosing appropriate staff who have the patience and personality to deal with challenging behaviour is critical – hanging on to them once found is vital. Communication and clarity is essential and regular self-evaluation is all important – 'it's as simple as that', he says, as he sits at a desk as a consultant, nowhere near the action in the field.

To summarize, the key factors for children with behaviour issues are:

- clearly specified rules
- expectations and instructions, along with frequent intermediate and consistent feedback on behaviour and redirection to task
- reasonable and meaningful consequences for both compliance and non-compliance will be necessary, along with adults who will deal with his or her issues based on knowledge, compassion and respect.

2. Teaching and learning targets
These are of primary importance for the prevention of challenging behaviour but all too often become secondary to the need to deal with the issues of the day.

Though by themselves such targets are usually insufficient to prevent many of the issues, if children are working on subjects they enjoy and in which they are encouraged to learn skills they feel they will benefit from both now and in the future, then, in theory, life would be sweet. Personalized learning objectives for every child is the goal for all schools and as such are on the top of everyone's agenda.

Having said this, I believe that students with challenging behaviour perhaps often need less personalized subject learning, at least initially, than do traditional learners. Though this may fly in the face of most conventional approaches, I believe that initially the key is to teach them not what to learn but how to learn it. Therefore personalization of learning, certainly in terms of study skills, is the starting point from which subject differentiation may develop – not the other way round.

3. Behaviour expectations and application of rules

The vital area of developing systems applying to all children and the design and development of behaviour expectations will be through formation of rules. This has three key components:

- the consistency of application of agreed rules by all stakeholders in the school
- the success of rewards and sanctions options to support agreed behaviour expectations and rules
- the process of continued development of key behaviour expectations and rules by all stakeholders in the school.

Schools will always need a degree of autonomy as to how they produce and organize their rules; they should, however, be devised in order of seriousness. An example of a priority schedule could be as follows for secondary school students:

(1) Completion of work and tasks.
(2) No physical or verbal aggression towards others.
(3) Use of mobile phones, etc., reflected in school policy.
(4) No eating or drinking in class.

(5) Timekeeping.
(6) Uniform or dress code, if there is one.

There will always be five to six key rules that all children should observe and little or no compromise should exist whatever diagnostic label a child may have in mainstream schools; this is especially so regarding verbal or physical aggression. With younger children the key rules are more likely to be based on social skills but initially they should be limited to a small definitive number and be as specific as possible.

Other areas to consider regarding rules are:

- Are they fresh?
- Do you have less than eight of them?
- Are they positively phrased?
- Are they fit for purpose?
- Have they been agreed by all?

Key rules should be devised by adherring to a stage-type process involving the following;

Stage 1: Agree upon the rules with the children; also agree consequences and rewards.
Stage 2: Gain commitment from parents/home supervisors.
Stage 3: Review and reconsider the rules.

One area that does need to be considered is that all children do not necessarily need to follow all the rules to the same extent. This is not fair, I hear you cry, but what if the reason is quite simply that

'Some of the children will follow all of the rules all of the time' and also . . .

'All of the children will follow some of the rules some of the time'

but you will never get . . .

'All of the students following all of the rules all of the time'?
The subset we are taking about is the group that follows some of the rules most of the time. They will need flexibility in some

areas, and if this does not seem fair it is because fairness is not giving every child the same – it is giving them what they need. The following is a suggested banding of rules that provide children with challenging behaviour the degree of flexibility they might require.

Band 1	Band 2
Physical/verbal abuse	Distractibility
Theft	Disorganization
Substance abuse	Calling out
Attendance/timekeeping	Fidgeting
Dress code/phone use	Engaging others

In such a model there should be little or no compromise regarding the agreed rules in Band 1 whether the child has ADHD, ODD, or is simply OTT (if you are wondering, 'Over The Top'). Band 2 is possibly where some flexibility could occur, especially if they are struggling to keep the rules in Band 1 in check. In my view, specific children may need a time span to develop those skills that other children naturally have in terms of ability to sit still, having all materials to hand, and being able to interact at the appropriate time.

Most teachers think that being flexible is not possible as the other students feel that the teacher is giving in to those who infringe in terms of disorganization and calling out. However it is worth mentioning that it is likely that the students know that others within the group are 'different learners'. Also, they will be observing the teacher's management approach regarding these different learners. In contrast, they will assess a rigid approach towards some of their peers that evidently does not work to be an indication that the teacher really has no clue about managing them. An adaptive approach to a situation that actually changes the outcome will be much more powerful.

4. General classroom management
This in itself is a huge subject and we are mainly going to cover it in relation to the issue of flexibility with regards to some of

the issues mentioned in Band 2, such as certain aspects of attention-seeking behaviour like calling out, fooling about, fidgeting, and lacking organizational skills.

To be fair to teachers, some of the issues mentioned above do 'nag away' and no matter how patient they may be these types of actions can be frustrating to deal with five days a week and almost 200 days a year. So, in order to respond to this, let us now look at three types of behaviour which could well be said to fit this low-level disruption description and which some children may well display in the classroom. The three types of behaviour are:

- fidgeting and restlessness
- attention-seeking behaviour
- organizational skills.

In each of these cases the key issue will be the attitude of the teacher towards the child displaying the behaviour. Let us look at some examples of how we could consider these areas.

FIDGETING AND RESTLESSNESS
The first question to ask is: why are they doing it? Is it because they are nervous, bored with the lesson, trying to avoid the task set, or need to be 'doing something' to help them stay engaged? Also, are they actually aware that they are doing it? Once you have isolated the main cause, strategies can then be employed. For example, for those not aware, a simple role-play exercise can illustrate the impact they are having on the teacher and the rest of the class. Or, for those who cannot help themselves, methods of getting them to monitor themselves can also be effective.

Obviously methods that reduce the temptation to play with equipment on desks can be effective so teachers could, for example, insist that all materials stay in bags placed on the floor until they need to be used, or in personal pencil cases. In younger classes pen tidies in central desk arrangements, files or trays can be used to store things away from busy hands.

Overall, a tidy and organized classroom with desks and chairs neatly arranged and rearranged throughout the day is effective. I used to always follow the mantra that 'Clutter is stress'.

Finally, if the child needs to fiddle, give them something to fiddle with, or allow them to doodle – it may be necessary to give them a scrap piece of paper. As for what to fiddle with, I used to allow some of the students to use a couple of small magnets. However, wristbands, or even pieces of Lego, can be effective. It's a case of trial and error, as you obviously do not want the item to be misused, or to be used as a weapon.

ATTENTION–SEEKING BEHAVIOUR

The key element of addressing attention-seeking behaviour is once again to focus on the message behind the behaviour and to see whether it is more a cry for help or a child not understanding the impact of their interruptions rather than a more concentrated plot to disrupt the class. Strategies here really are down to the teacher setting the tone of how the class will be run and by which and what means children will be able to communicate with them and with each other during time spent in the room. Once again, consistency and fairness will determine the outcome, as well as the teacher's management style.

Strategies that I have found work best include the following.

- Asking for everybody's attention and not starting until you get it, or waiting for as long as it takes even if it means sitting at your desk or looking at your watch and marking the minutes on the board.
- Dealing firmly and non-emotionally with, for example, somebody swinging on a chair, as in the following example: 'Alfie, don't swing on the chair, it's not safe and it is not allowed.'

'But, Sir, I want to,' Alfie replies.

'Ok, it's your choice, but if you want to be on two legs you can stand and work and I will take the chair away . . . if you want to use the chair, it has four legs, and that's the rule.'

End of story

Another way of managing attention-seeking behaviour, rather than dealing with it verbally, is to use your own presence by moving near to the child on those occasions that you think warrant this approach. Simply standing behind or beside the child can often dampen the activity level of the individual quite dramatically, without a word being spoken regarding the behaviour.

One technique that I think does not work too well but is often mentioned in textbooks is that of tactically ignoring attention-seeking behaviour. In my experience it is always better to acknowledge the issue as ignoring it more often inflames or accelerates a greater response. However, as in most cases, it is not what you do but how you do it. In some situations if the actions are not affecting the class as a whole 'a knowing look', or a quick response that makes it clear that this is not relevant to the issue right now, can be enough. If only you or a few children appear affected by actions which are more covert, a quick tap on the shoulder and a word in the ear that you will catch up with them later may be enough.

If the actions are more disruptive and are affecting the class, meet the situation with a firm but businesslike approach, explaining that this is not the required level of behaviour at this time; then give only one warning that, if repeated, consequences will occur. *One* warning, not two.

In addition, try to model the appropriate behaviour of other students and also – yes, go on and be inclusive – try to involve those potentially 'disruptive but different' children as much as possible even if you feel they don't really know the correct answers. As always in your communication with them, use language that is positive and firm, but friendly.

Finally, praise for appropriate responses will always be a welcome option, and involving the rest of the class – getting them to help the children with ADHD and to help in process by '*not* winding them up' or provoking them into being the class clown – can be very helpful.

If all else fails bribery is always an option, provided it is accompanied by flexible and proactive management. One teacher I know who had a particularly challenging child would, when the student had had a good lesson, let him play a game on his phone for the last five minutes of the class. Did the other children say 'this was not fair' . . . no, they didn't, as they understood that what the teacher was doing was in the interests of the whole class.

ORGANIZATIONAL SKILLS

This too is an area in which I strongly believe teachers need to be more flexible. Unfortunately, I have witnessed so many occasions where issues have accelerated into major confrontations, for example, begining with an exasperated teacher shouting 'David, where is your pen?' It is so true that for many students with ADHD and ODD it is not so much the issue of what to learn but how to learn it. Study skills, or learning to learn skills, really is a key role in achieving teaching success, whether pupils are five or 15.

My advice to staff dealing with these children in situations such as the above is to keep an extra set of pens, and other educational materials, in the classroom. If possible, few, if any, items should go with students when they leave the lesson.

Regarding homework, I advise that textbooks do not leave the school but that the child should have assignments photocopied or a second set of books and materials at home. The same principle should apply to clothing for sports, etc., where a second set or backup set should always be left in school as a contingency. Using a study buddy or peer mentor to help children get to lessons on time and not be distracted when travelling between classes, and in other areas of organisation, may also be an option.

Flexibility

Though structure is vital, the key element in achieving success with challenging children is the ability to provide a large degree of flexibility in the management of behaviour. Within the context of the school environment therefore, the following areas are important in achieving positive results:

- Differentiation
- Management of rewards and sanctions
- Management systems for non-structured time
- Looking at alternative skills pathways
- Working with multi-agencies.

Differentiation

Although we covered teaching and learning targets in the previous section of this chapter, that element of curriculum management related to planning. Differentiation relates to execution (of the work outcomes, not the child, however tempting that may sound).

Differentiation, as stated by Eyre (2001), is 'recognizing individual differences and trying to find institutional strategies which take account of them'. Although the word will mean different things to different people, various components of differentiation need to take place:

Outcome – the setting of common tasks which can be responded to in a positive way by all pupils.

Input – the setting of different tasks at different levels of difficulty for different levels of achievement.

Task – requiring greater sophistication within a common theme or topic allowing pupils to contribute as individuals and collaboratively to the input and so raise standards of output for all pupils in the group.

Enrichment – giving pupils supplementary tasks intended to broaden and deepen skills and understanding.

Pace – having different expectations of the pace at which different children will complete the task.

Resources – providing different levels of resources and information.

Rate of progress – allowing pupils to proceed through a course at their own speed.

Variety – using different teaching strategies versus different learning styles.

Management of rewards and sanctions

One of the most contentious issues in the management of children with behaviour problems is the use of rewards and sanctions. There still appears to be a strong belief that children with challenging behaviour need discipline through sanctions as that 'will learn them'. Rewards should be for good behaviour and performance it is true, but in reality rewards also affect long–term change in behaviour while sanctions may in practice only hold the behaviour in check for a short time.

In practice, however, both should be used in combination but the ratio should differ with different types of student; for example, rewards are far more likely to work with children with ADHD, than are sanctions. The reason for this is that children with ADHD have a very short-term memory which needs constant stimulation and therefore it is easier to stimulate positive responses through rewards rather than sanctions which usually have a timescale before they can be enforced. The ratio of rewards to sanctions should probably be in the region of 75 per cent rewards to 25 per cent sanctions. Students with CD are more premeditated and therefore more likely be in control of their responses to situations. As a result, they are more likely to respond to a more even approach of rewards and sanctions, perhaps a ratio of 50 per cent rewards and 50 per cent sanctions. Students with Oppositional Defiant Disorder lie somewhere in the middle between ADHD and CD. As a result, the ratio should be in the region of 65 per cent rewards to 35 per cent sanctions.

When asking yourself why the students in your class do the work you provide and do what they are told when they are told to, one further question you should be asking is what is in it for them? Or why do they do it? For the majority, the incentive or goal is more long term; they are playing the school game, which means positive actions and results will allow them options in the future, for example, parent satisfaction regarding their performance, or pathways to college or a career.

Children with challenging behaviour do not play the long game; they play a short game. They need the reward or incentive now. They are not looking to the future – the risk factors mentioned earlier in this book have seen to that.

Rewards therefore, must be more immediate. The trick is to infer more which incentives work, as I believe that in most cases everybody has 'their price'.

The following are examples of rewards:

- commendations/merits/certificates/tokens
- positive comments
- contact with home
- trips
- freedom of movement
- video/computer options
- choice of lesson options
- earning of other responsibilities
- specific systems, contracts, phone credits, food or money credits.

Obviously the age and type of school will determine which incentives will be used but over the years I have used everything from 'Praise to Money'. I am not recommending you give them money yourself, but if giving money is a valid price, and the setting up of a system can be arranged, then do it. An example of how this can take place is through specialist contracts, which are explained in the next chapter.

One last thing regarding rewards, however, is that it is not always the reward itself that may be the most important issue for the individual, but who gives it to them. This point leads us to sanctions, whereby disappointing a particular supervisor who has a good relationship with the child can be the most powerful sanction of all. Having said that, other options that are listed below can be effective, especially with students with CD who need a planned programme of management that contract systems can sometimes provide. Possible sanctions include:

- shouting/displeasure of supervisor
- loss of merits/privileges

- removal from a specific place/class to another area
- whole-class sanctions
- detentions/loss of freedom of movement
- contact with home
- contracts with home and/or multi-agency.

Though we will be looking at some multi-agency contracts later on, the key is that they are given early in the process or else some students will wear them as a badge of honour within the gang, as in 'I've got an ASBO [Anti-Social Behaviour Order] what have you got?'

Management systems for non-structured time
One of the crucial areas that will reinforced in any successful management process will be non-structured time. Options for all sorts of negative interactions take place on the way to and from school and during break and lunchtime. Failure to think about ways of providing improved supervision of specific individuals during this time will invariably undo much of the work being provided elsewhere in the school.

Obviously the variables offered by these non-structured times can include everything from low-level mischief to full-scale bullying and extortion. The key, as always, is to be proactive rather than reactive, getting in first, and trying to predict where potential flashpoints might occur. Easier said than done – but whoever said this job was easy?

Looking at alternative skills pathways
Looking again at the issue of why children learn throws up some interesting points about what they learn and where they learn it. Though we have been working on the inclusive system for some years now, it is clear that particular children will need sets of skills and training that are different to those offered by the conventional curriculum and often a more non-traditional set-up in which to gain them.

Though the ages of children, the policies and the culture of specific institutions will be factors in how and which alternative skills pathways can be provided for individuals, if we are really serious about dealing with challenging behaviour it is patently clear that a 'one size fits all' school system approach is not going to work, especially for children with CD. Options include looking at more practical skills within the 3Cs area for teenage boys, i.e. 'construction, cooking and cars', but variations of different skills pathways for both boys and girls at all stages of their child development need to be explored alongside the use of Learning Support Units and Nurture groups within the school.

Working with multi-agencies
For some students, the need to provide a system to regularly identify targets and to measure progress towards these targets will need a more structured approach. The type and range of agencies involved will be determined by the specific issues encountered but for some time now schools have been used to working in the context of a multi-agency approach. However, the range of options available can be quite difficult to coordinate, especially if many agencies are involved.

It is to be hoped that the principles and practices of the Every Child Matters policy, which highlights the need for a lead professional across the agencies involved with a specific child, will provide better communication and cooperation than in the past. However, the proof of this particular policy pudding will be in the eating.

The 3Rs
To sell, support and sustain structure and flexibility working in tandem, we need Respect, Relationships and Role Models in mananaging challenging behaviour.

Respect
Obvious to say, but as pointed out earlier in practice sometimes it is difficult to always like children with challenging behaviour, who appear to make no attempt to try to have a positive relationship with you.

Though it is not always easy, teachers need to adopt the principle of disassociating the behaviour from the child, and it is worth revisiting the point that it is the negative behaviour that you don't like, not the child. If the child, especially one with ODD, ever gets a smell of the fact that you don't like *them* then it will be very hard to work this out with them in the future. As a result it is worth considering the following points:

- teachers of more challenging children must first assess their own feelings when working with these students
- the way in which teachers behave towards any child often influences the way that other children react towards the child
- how teachers use their power over students.

Selling the reasons why someone should turn up on time and spend up to six hours a day five days a week and up to 200 days a year in one particular place, especially if they do what they like the rest of the time outside the school, is not easy. Without some sort of emotional handle or bond between teacher and children progress will be limited.

On this issue of respect or self-respect, that could be said to be wrapped up in self-esteem, it may be worth considering what it means to have self-esteem. Although everybody will have their own version of what self-esteem is, I have often found it is to do with fear of failure, or not being to deal with failure. Confidence in yourself appears to mean that if you fail on a particular occasion, you will put things right next time. This is why I feel so many children with low self-esteem explode when challenged – it is a reaction at not feeling able to change things next time.

Having made the above points, the building of respect should be initiated by the teacher. But respect must be reciprocated at some point by the pupil. We cannot go down a one-way street with only one party trying to make things happen. Children who do not or will not work with a teacher acting correctly within this framework will ultimately find themselves facing less and less flexibility regarding the management of their behaviour.

Relationships

To support challenging behaviour a number of relationships need to be forged within the school environment. These include:

- teacher–pupil interaction
- relationships with other members of staff
- pupil–pupil interaction
- teacher–parent relationships.

Though positive relationships with all children are obviously to be encouraged, it is often the case that in practice it may be difficult to forge a relationship with particular pupils with whom you may just not click. In cases such as these it remains vitally important to keep things as positive as possible and to this end use of language in communication is all important. Some examples of the positive use of language in specific situations are listed below.

Following instructions

'Thanks for doing this stuff, I asked you to do this and you are doing it.'
'When I look at this room I see poetry in motion.'
'I asked you to do this and you have remembered the instructions.'
'I know you hate this rule but you are doing it anyway.'
'You worked this out on your own didn't you?'

Working on something the child finds difficult

'You didn't give up and you got the problem sorted.'
'I know you find this difficult but I can see you are trying. You have already done four questions.'
'I know you don't get this but you are still trying, as I can see.'
'I see you asked Jamie for help when you got stuck; that was a good piece of initiative.'

Accepting another person's point of view

'Even though I know you have a strong opinion on this you are letting others have their say.'

'I know you think it is unfair but thanks for letting Ruth go first.'

'You took on board the idea/situation/instruction, even at first I could see you didn't agree.'

Despite everything it is often the case that children with challenging behaviour need to establish relationships with a variety of other staff in order to try to support the systems that they may feel are stacked against them. Sometimes the child (usually unfairly) sees the person or an individual teacher as the problem and will not listen or comply with anything that person will say or do. In this and in other cases it is important that someone else acts as a listener and also an alternative person selling the message of positive choices with regards to learning and behaviour.

It is ironic but true that children sometimes accept the same instructions from another person who they feel is on their side. Although no such thing as sides exist, it is as if the student's perception of other members of staff, including learning mentors, counsellors, student coaches and often the learning support assistant, is that only they can operate in a place where teachers cannot tread. This is yet another example of flexible thinking in getting the job done, and specifics points on the roles of some of these professionals will be covered in later chapters.

Another area of relationship building or supporting positive learning and behaviour is peer mentoring, which will also be covered in the following chapters.

Pupil–pupil interaction itself remains another crucial area for behavioural outcomes. I once did a project as part of my Masters degree on the reasons why children came to school to learn and one of the main conclusions I came to is that they come to meet their friends. As a result pupil–pupil relationships is an extremely powerful area of influence and obviously this can be for both positive and negative reasons. However, it is a difficult area for adults to manage, especially when adolescence begins as you cannot dictate the relationships pupils will have.

Having said this, the plan should always include ways of looking at improving the understanding and acceptance of differences between individuals. Ways of doing this would include:

- class team building
- Circle Time options
- PSHE/Citizenship
- drama
- role-play
- peer mediation.

Finally, parents remain the greatest influence on child behaviour and any system, if it is to work, must include parents in the plan. Though we will talk at length about the role of parents in later chapters, the key issue regarding parents and challenging behaviour is *communication* between school and home. The better the communication, the better the outcome. Though this is easier said than done, failure to prepare to do this is likely to prepare you to fail.

Ways of conducting communication include:

- frequent telephone/text/email contact
- frequent parent–teacher conferences
- frequent report cards.

However, children with behavioural issues can place a great deal of pressure on family relationships so bear in mind that:

- parents may require parenting skills input
- parents must try to look after themselves
- in persistently difficult situations co-existing parental SEN issues should be considered.

Regular meetings may also be required and for these helpful tips include the following:

- Listen and acknowledge – allow them to express themselves uninterrupted.
- Ask them what they think they need in order to resolve the issue.
- Agree to reasonable requests. Consider when and who will action them.
- Add any further elements to the solution when you feel they are necessary.
- Give the parent(s) a clear and realistic date when you will contact them and tell them about progress.
- Thank them and remind them that you have their child's best interest at heart.

Keep meetings to a maximum of 45 minutes. If you cannot resolve the issue in that time then arrange another meeting. If a time limit is not applied the overly sympathetic teacher may well find the meeting will run and run until the teacher knows the complete history of the child and of the parents as well.

Role models
Remember our Scottish teacher early in the chapter? Such teachers can be a good role model for pupils. In some cases the child may not have particularly good role models in his or her life. Finding alternative, positive role models can be very important for all children but especially so for children with CD. Factors determining your reputation as a role model in relation to pupil behaviour will include:

- the way you present yourself and the reputation you acquire
- the tone and boundaries that you set
- the consistency of your discipline
- the way in which you personalize your teaching and hone your skills in the production of interesting and entertaining lessons.

What students usually need from their teacher is SF3R. You can achieve this through the 3Fs – being Firm, Fair and Funny – by following core characteristics within a positive setting.

Behaviour Management – Characteristics of Schools and Teachers

Characteristics of schools

- Active participation throughout the lesson.
- A good extracurricular programme where children can develop their strengths away from their academic studies. Some children are often very keen to take art or contribute to sporting activities and team games, although individual sports such as swimming may be more suitable.
- Methods of grouping children that allows them to learn most effectively while protecting their self-esteem
- Streaming, whether by ability or method, of some children can help a child feel comfortable in an environment suited to his or her needs.
- A special educational needs department that has an understanding of behaviour issues.
- A calm, encouraging and consistent approach, with a well-structured routine, clear rules and standards of work both in school and for homework.
- Traditional closed-plan rooms rather than an open, less structured environment.
- Teachers who are always present and not called away to other duties during the school day.
- Teachers at ease talking to parents.

Characteristics of teachers

- Clearly tell children what they want them to do and not what they don't want them to do.
- Model the particular behaviour they wish to establish (don't expect it to magically occur).
- Specify a specific consequence (i.e. a sanction for inappropriate behaviour and consistently follow though, mean what you say and say what you mean).
- Consistently reward appropriate, or sanction inappropriate, behaviour.

- Recognize that every child has 'their price' and establish what it is in terms of appropriate rewards and sanctions that work for them.
- Are specific when directing verbal responses to both appropriate and inappropriate behaviours.
- Establish non-verbal 'response cost' systems with specific children.
- Withdraw attention from annoying/irritating behaviours, if possible.
- Allow volatile individuals an 'escape hatch' in terms of response to inappropriate behaviour – if possible, do not confront.
- Use humour to deflect, detract and diffuse situations.

6 Troubleshooting in Action: Behaviour Action Contracts

If it was not made clear in the previous chapter, I would reinforce the point that in order to maintain structure and the systems of structure, flexibility is the key component. Schools and teachers of challenging students have for many years used a range of strategies to encourage the cooperation of those who find it difficult to work within the regular system. One strategy is the use of student behavioural contracts.

Such contracts are not a new concept but in this chapter we are going to look at a process of devising a strategy to improve behaviour by use of a behavioural contract with a twist. I call this strategy a Behaviour Action Contract, which as explained below, to be adapted for use in different schools.

Though this contract can be used in different ways for a variety of students and reasons, cases where it will usually work best are those students who fit into the ADHD and ODD categories discussed previously and are at risk of class withdrawal or possible school exclusion. Though it may work for students with CD, the main motivation here is to try to help children who cannot help themselves as opposed to those who may help themselves most of the time and do this very well (but this is a personal opinion with which many of you may disagree).

Contracts to some extent often have a negative tone when it comes to behaviour as they can be seen as preparing a paper trail to justify or record incidents for use in potential exclusion options, etc. The other side of the coin, however, is that for some individuals and their families they can provide a daily record of events and can focus minds on the immediate tasks of achieving targets, which can be helped by regular input and feedback.

The other area, as mentioned before, and which will be contentious, is that treating some children in a different way is not fair on those who behave in a traditional manner. Again, I maintain that fairness is not equal and equal is not fair. Some children need a more immediate set of incentives in order to work within the school system.

Behaviour Action Contracts: The Process

In the case of a child who is appearing to offer many challenges the following steps and approaches might be followed.

STAGE 1
An initial meeting should initially take place between the child and the form tutor or head of year, department head, headteacher, or other appropriate person. Whoever is responsible will be the designated 'Contract Manager' and an open discussion about the issues of concern should take place.

In this meeting, a list of not more than five specific areas of concern or poor behaviours should be outlined as target areas for improvement to be agreed between the student and the Contract Manager. The key factor is to try to make the issues as specific as possible. Some examples could be:

- Swearing in class
- Late to school/class
- Defiance of a particular teacher
- Verbally or physically abusing a specific student
- Not following the dress code.

From these five concerns or behaviours, at least two should be picked out that will act as specific target behaviours. This should take place after some negotiation between the Contract Manager and the child, and while it is good to have an open and honest dialogue about the choice, some direction should be given by the supervisor, though advising the child to improve in all five areas could be alluded to. The principle here is that in practice it is often impossible to work on multiple behaviour targets and it is often more pragmatic for a child to concentrate on two specific issues. Also, what often happens is that once in the contract mode, other related difficulties tend to diminish. However, certain individuals will always play or try to beat the system and we will come to these later. In addition, at this time the child should identify a peer mentor or another child in the school or organization who will be involved in this process. In the best-case scenario the peer mentor would be chosen by the contracted child, but in cases where the Contract Manager does not agree on the choice then the contracted child should have opportunity for some input into who is chosen. This is a vital stage in the process and without a peer mentor or another child acting as an ongoing adviser under the scheme many children following the contract option fail. There is no doubt that in practice this is often a major stumbling block as the choice of the other child can be difficult due to the interests and the particular position of the challenging child within the school community.

Quite often the peer mentor will be a member of the school council who is seen as 'all right', and not a nerd or 'sucker up' but it might be a more self-sufficient friend of the pupil and, better still, an older sibling. Though some scepticism may exist among those of you reading this, in practice this works and to a certain extent you have to 'suck it and see'.

From hereon, the Contract Manager will have telephone contact with the parents and will invite them to a meeting to discuss STAGE 2.

STAGE 2
Once Stage 1 has been followed through the child is now ready to enter into the contract, which will be presented to the child and parents at a meeting at the school organized by the Contract Manager. The focus here is to finalize the two specific issues

under consideration and discuss the mechanics of recording and the evaluation of successful outcomes.

At this time the Behaviour Action Card will be shown to both the parents and the child, the Card being the tool for measuring the performance of the child in practical terms. It will be explained that the Behavioiur Action Card is the main tool for staff to use to record whether the child has been able to achieve the criteria expected during both class and non-structured time.

Two points can be awarded per class attendance: one point for each of the two issues, the teacher's signature being required in each class. It will be explained that points can be added or docked by the Contract Manager for issues that present themselves outside of the classroom environment. The role of the peer mentor and the parents is to make sure that each day they have seen a record of the child's performance and they must sign the card each day.

The concept of achieving a Gold, Siver or Bronze standard will be explained to both the parents and the child, and it will be explained how points can be converted into a money reward option.

The parties involved, namely the child, parents and supervisor, along with the peer mentor, then sign the Behaviour Action Contract. The peer mentor will not attend the whole meeting but will be introduced after the initial discussions with the parents and the contracted student have taken place.

A timescale for a review of the situation will be discussed. In most cases this will be a period of two weeks, but a degree of flexibility may be required here.

Flexibility should be a feature of all aspects of this approach (the above is only a suggested course of action). In some cases it may be that concentrating on a specific issue will be sufficient and the appropriate course. In this case the Behaviour Action Card could be adapted to show just one daily point for the target achieved, or one could keep to the two points if a graduated response to the issue is considered a more workable approach.

An example of a Behaviour Action Contract and a Behaviour Action Card are given at the end of this chapter.

STAGE 3

Once agreement has taken place all staff will need to be informed of the nature of the contact by the Contract Manager and of the requirement that they have to complete and sign a Behaviour Action Card for each day the child attends their class. In addition, though they do not need to know exactly what the points will result in and how the mechanics of the contract work, fuller details should be available to staff from the Contract Manager.

In practice, the role of the Contract Manager is central to the success of this scheme, as is the role of parents. In addition, it is essential to adapt the concept for both specific students and particular schools.

However, although no hard and fact rules can or should be applied, the following guidance and suggestions may prove helpful.

- The scheme is not based on a Monday to Friday system but over a five-day period comprising when those five days occur.
- A meeting with all teaching staff involved with the student should take place to establish some degree of consistency of action with regards to measurement of target issues.
- Teaching staff, whatever their personal views, must be objective and committed to the scheme (easier said than done!)

- The Card is the responsibility of the student. If he or she loses it or cannot find it, no points will be awarded for that day or that lesson.
- The Card should not be used to offset other possible rewards or sanctions that apply to other pupils. This is an extra incentive, agreed between the school, parents and the pupil.
- The Contract Manager and peer mentor should be in regular contact and be active in helping the contracted child wherever possible.

Disadvantages of the scheme

There is no doubt that operating such a process takes up a lot of precious time; however, alternative approaches for students who are struggling with their behavour will usually not offset this particular point as behaviour management, whether it is exclusion or classroom withdrawal, etc., eats up time.

Another main potential problem is specific children taking advantage of the opportunity to play the system and therefore the scheme will not be suitable for those who are patently able or likely to be premeditated to do so. It is likely, however, that such individuals need a much more directed multi-agency approach in any case.

The biggest stumbling block in practice, however, will be the attitudes of staff, who will see the scheme as rewarding poor behaviour. This is the one issue that is very difficult to address in practice . . . other than to ask what alternative approach they would propose for a child who is in major danger of class withdrawal or exclusion.

Advantages of the scheme

We know that rewards change behaviour and sanctions don't. The question is what rewards are tangible for certain individuals and the truth is that schools do not offer the rewards that some children with challenging behaviour value. Nor should schools in my opinion provide money, phone tokens, etc., for what is traditional behaviour values. This is not what schools should be doing

– for most children the rewards that schools do offer in terms of providing education, skills, advice, individual merit and team rewards are perfectly adequate.

Having said this, for schools to get the job done some individuals will need an extra incentive, and the advantage of this scheme lies not really in what the child will get but in who is involved in the process of giving it to them. It is not the money or the phone tokens that is the reward; it is the fact that the three sets of people involved in the process along with the child are likely to be those that have most influence on them, namely the Contract Manger, another child who they may respect, and their parents.

The true value of the reward is that the Behaviour Action Card can help focus the child on certain aspects of their behaviour, not because of material reward but hopefully because of the relationships with those involved in the process.

Try it, and see what I mean!

Example of Behaviour Action Contract

Students at this school/organization are committed to behaving in an acceptable manner.

To help students make the positive choices necessary to improve their educational goals, a **Behaviour Action Contract** is agreed between the student, the school, the parent/carers and a designated Peer Mentor.

This contract is made on: (date)............................
Name of student:..
Date of birth.......................... Class/Year.....................
Address..
....

I (name) .... agree the following regarding my future behaviour:

* **Target 1: I agree to...**
* **Target 2: I agree to...**

I (parent's name) .... will undertake the following to assist in the improvement of .... behaviour:

Student............ School Representative ....
Parent/Carer..........................Peer Mentor.....................

Review Date ....

Example of Behaviour Action Card

	Day 1 Points/ Initials 0/1/2		Day 2 Points/ Initials 0/1/2		Day 3 Points/ Initials 0/1/2		Day 4 Points/ Initials 0/1/2		Day 5 Points/ Initials 0/1/2	
Lesson 1										
Lesson 2										
Lesson 3										
Lesson 4										
Lesson 5										
Lesson 6										
Dock										
Bonus										
Total										
Peer Mentor										
Form Teacher										
Parent										

Student's name_____Start date _____
Behavioural issues_____
and_____

Note: Docking of or bonus points added by Form Teacher or Contract Manager

Points calculation

5-day worksheet that is *not* always M–F	5 lessons		6 lessons		7 lessons		8 lessons	
	5-day total min-imum points	Min-imum daily points	5-day total min-imum points	Min-imum daily points	5-day total min-imum points	Min-imum daily points	5-day total min-imum points	Min-imum daily points
Gold	45	9	55	11	60	12	65	13
Silver	40	8	45	9	55	11	60	12
Bronze	35	7	40	8	45	9	55	11

Points converted into rewards

Suggested costing of money or money equivalent for 5-day period

	16+	12–15	8–11	4–7
Gold	£15.00	£10.00	£7.50	£5.00
Silver	£10.00	£7.50	£5.00	£3.75
Bronze	£7.50	£5.00	£3.75	£2.50

Suggested costing of money or money equivalent per day

	16+	12–15	8–11	4–7
Gold	£3.00	£2.00	£1.50	£1.00
Silver	£2.00	£1.50	£1.00	£.75
Bronze	£1.50	£1.00	£.75	£.50

7 Troubleshooting in Action: Bullying and Anger Management

In this chapter we are going to look at two key areas that affect all schools to some degree: the issue of bullying, and dealing with children who require anger management.

What is Bullying?

Bullying can be defined as 'aggressive or insulting behaviour by an individual or group often repeated over a period of time that intentionally hurts or harms' (Ofsted 2003). It involves some imbalance in power, and its effect on individuals differs according to personality and the perceived severity of the incidents. For some, bullying can produce feelings of helplessness and isolation, undermine self-esteem and affect school performance. In the most severe cases it can lead to serious distress and long-term damage to social and emotional development.

How Common Is bullying?

There remains debate about how common bullying is in schools and much depends upon individual perceptions of what constitutes bullying behaviour. Behaviour that the school may define as unpleasant, aggressive or unkind, victims may see as bullying. In many studies the incidence of bullying has always been seen as being much higher by pupils than by schools. In a 1998/99 Home Office report, a third of 12 to 16-year-old pupils surveyed reported being bullied at school in the previous year. Research carried out by Smith (1999) indicated that between 10 to 20 per cent of pupils interviewed felt they had been bullied in the six months before the survey.

Homophobic Bullying

Ofsted's report *Sex and Relationships* (2002) recommends that schools must be prepared to challenge homophobia and encourage pupils to respect differences in sexuality in order to reject prejudice and homophobic bullying. Perceived homosexuality is the second most likely trigger for bullying after weight, and reports suggest that gay and lesbian adolescents are at least twice as likely to commit suicide as their heterosexual peers.

What Can Schools Do To Reduce Bullying?

Disputes regarding what behaviour constitutes bullying, and realistic expectations regarding the school's ability to stop it occurring, often cause tension between parents and schools. The common factor in bullying, as opposed to other levels of pupil disagreements, is the repetitive and intentional nature of behaviour that is aimed at undermining an individual by highlighting a difference or vulnerability in order to establish control. The increased focus upon the rights of all children to be kept safe and free from harm has highlighted the need for all members of a school's community to take action to reduce the likelihood of bullying. This suggests that schools should begin by consulting and liaising with parents and pupils in order to share a definition of what bullying is and communicate this to all. It needs to be understood that action undertaken by the school alone is unlikely to impact upon bullying significantly, although it may reduce its occurrence on school premises.

Action to reduce bullying

The following actions and approaches can contribute to significantly reducing bullying.

- The production and monitoring of an effective and proactive anti-bullying policy that is implemented consistently and that identifies clear success criteria. The policy must result from collaboration and consultation with children, parents and staff, to promote ownership by all.

- A strong school ethos that promotes tolerance, including respect for difference and diversity, in order to create a school culture where prejudice, harassment and humiliation are rejected. This might suggest increasing children's awareness of other cultures through PSHE and citizenship, exploring issues relating to sexuality, and debate regarding equal opportunities.

- Positive leadership on monitoring bullying incidents and clear and consistently applied procedures that indicate expectations regarding attitudes and behaviour. This may involve appointing a member of the senior management team with responsibility for reducing bullying incidence and raising the profile of anti-bullying strategies within the school.

- Effective ways of reducing any identified cause of bullying, for example establishing money-free environments, not allowing valuables to be brought to school, a clear policy on designer clothing, etc.

- Having school polices and procedures that demonstrate and model acceptance and unconditional valuing of all members of the school community, despite differences and disabilities. Ensuring that this is modelled in staff–staff interaction, child–staff interaction and parent–staff interaction.

- Having in place policies to reduce and deal with incidence of bullying that focus upon specific group, for example race and sexuality. Monitoring the effectiveness of the policies by assessing data on bullying incidents.

- Raising of bullying issues in curriculum areas such as English and PE, with specific programmes aimed at raising issues implemented in subjects such as citizenship, PSHE and drama.

- Increasing staff awareness of bullying and taking appropriate action to reduce it. The latter may include rigorous supervision of the school site and particular vigilance in bullying hotspots that have been identified through regular consultation with pupils.

- Taking action to reject a 'no telling' climate in school, and to identify ways that encourage children to confide in order to bring issues to the attention of staff. Research indicates that children are more likely to confide concerns relating to bullying to other pupils, so peer supporters may be more effective than teachers.

- Research indicates that methods of dealing with bullying that promote a no-blame, conciliation and repatriation approach are generally more effective in encouraging disclosure and reducing bullying incidents than apportioning of blame and applying sanctions, although these may be required at times.

- Taking action to reduce peer compliance and duplicity in bullying incidents. This may be through employing theatre/art groups to explore issues and encourage a shared responsibility towards all members of the school community.

- Providing a sanctuary or quiet area for those who may feel vulnerable in less closely supervised periods.

- Deliberate action to break down age stratification. This might include mixed age houses or tutor groups, buddy systems and after-school clubs.

- The employment of child-centred devices to reduce the isolation that often accompanies bullying, such as Circle of Friends or buddies.

- Taking all bullying assertions seriously, and having in place action to support the immediate investigation of concerns when they arise. This could be supported by having a named contact for parents and/or children to discuss issues relating to bullying, and establishing a same-day response to concerns.

- Having in place procedures to reduce the chances that children will bully/be bullied. These may include social skills training and action to increase pupil empathy.

- Publicizing contact details such as local and national helplines aimed at reducing the impact of bullying. Supporting children's awareness through the availability of publications on bullying and its impact is also essential.

Supporting the Bullied

Individuals who are bullied can be from any ability range or from any social background, although they are more likely to be those who react in some way to the bullying behaviour. It is thought that it is the reaction that picks them out as a likely victim and that this response is often a repeated pattern in their later lives. Teaching assertiveness may help, as may encouraging them to avoid situations where bullying is more likely to take place. Ensuring that children feel they are not responsible – that being bullied does not signify a fault in them – can help to reduce self-blame. Having time to listen is important, and is encouraging all pupils to accept responsibility to report any incidents they have worries about, even if they are not directly involved, can have an impact.

Supporting the Bullies

Most pupils can bully if put in a situation where they perceive there to be a gain in power for them. National surveys note that half of those who bully had also at some time been bullied and although bullies can be from any background or ability range research suggests they are more likely to be those who are influenced by sub-cultures and peer/family experiences where bullying is acceptable. To demonize children who intimidate others does not support the reflection needed to change behaviour patterns. Responses from bullies suggest that in many cases they do not perceive their behaviour to be harmful. Responses such as 'We were only having a laugh, we were only teasing' are commonplace. A way forward must aim at developing processes that allow children to feel confident enough to discuss feelings, share experiences and develop empathy with others. Reports have suggested that pupils who bully may include those who fail to understand the relationship between behaviour and consequences. They may have had chaotic lives where the responses from significant others have been inconsistent and unpredictable. Sometimes they are popular and charismatic and bullying is a testing of the boundaries to assess the limits of the power they already have.

Parents can often react negatively to suggestions that their child is behaving in an inappropriate manner and evidence may be questioned or denied. For some parents this is a period of loss that needs time to adjust to and schools need to be careful in their choice of vocabulary when describing events by avoiding emotive terminology. The suggestion of blame that accompanies words such as bully, often results in denial and refusal to participate in processes aimed at reducing further incident. A more worthwhile approach might be to encourage shared responsibility to promote positive interaction, and working towards identifying a route that repairs the damage and makes repatriation easier.

Finally, always consider whether behaviour in school, such as put-downs of children, has been tolerated by staff – or even instigated by them – and this has been interpreted by pupils as a sign of acceptability. Light-hearted banter may be funny if it happens once, but many pupils and staff remain ignorant of the drip, drip effect this can have on pupils' self-esteem.

Anger Management

Anyone can become angry – that is easy. But to be angry with the right person to the right degree at the right time for the right purpose and in the right way – that is not easy

(Aristotle)

What is Anger?

Anger can be described as:

- A secondary emotion resulting from a primary emotion that presents a threat such as such as fear, disappointment, envy or injury.
- A reflection of an emotional difficulty, such as a diagnosed disorder.
- An instrumental behaviour that is intended to bring about submission or control.
- Catharsis to provide a release of emotions.

All of us experience anger. Anger can be a catalyst that provokes a reaction and allows change. Anger itself is not a problem, it is the behaviour that results from that anger that can be unacceptable and require modification.

Predisposing Factors
Elaine Douglas suggests that the predisposing factors that make it more likely that responses to anger are unacceptable are:

- Genetic and constitutional variables.
- Child-rearing factors such as parenting styles.
- Developmental factors – premature and low-weight babies, or early neglect/abuse.
- Personality traits shaped by environment and life experiences.
- Social-economic status, e.g. children from younger mothers are more at risk.
- Learned responses – early parental/carer models.
- Beliefs which affect attitudes and in turn affect behaviour.
- Life circumstances such as influences of peer pressure.

Understanding Anger

The firework model adapted from Novaco's model for Anger Arousal by Fiendler and Ecton (1986) is often used to demonstrate the processes associated with anger. The trigger is the match, the fuse the thoughts and feelings engendered, and the explosive cylinder is the body's reaction or behavioural response. This model can be usefully employed with pupils to assist them in understanding the processes involved.

Responses to Anger

When anger is being expressed the emotional mind can supersede the rational mind. The resulting behaviours can include:

- *Displacement*, when anger is externalized to some other person or object. This can be a positive response as it allows thinking time.

- *Repression*, when anger is pushed down and affects later unconscious behaviours.
- *Suppression*, when a deliberate attempt is made to hide anger. This may affect emotional health.
- *Ineffectual expression* of anger – usually hostile and aggressive behaviour, the flight or fight instinct.
- *Effective expression* of anger, when others' views are respected and there is a positive resolution of conflict.

There are three major perspectives in understanding anger. These are:

- *Behavioural perspectives* place the emphasis upon the *behaviour* itself and therefore uses techniques such as ABC for addressing difficulties. ABC concerns itself with identifying the **a**ntecedents that preceded the behaviour, the **b**ehaviour itself and the **c**onsequences of that behaviour. What was the pay-off for the individual concerned? The idea is that reducing/avoiding the antecedent can alter the resulting behaviour.
- *Psychoanalytical* perspectives place emphasis upon an individual's *feelings* and thoughts. It concentrates upon the influence of attachment and of establishing a secure emotional base in order to be able to respond adequately to situations.
- *Cognitive and behavioural* perspectives consider that it is the *thinking* that influences emotions. These thoughts then in turn drive the behavioural response. The solution in this case is to rationalize and change the thinking.

School Action

Any action taken to increase an individual's ability to react appropriately when they become angry must address the following:

- Acceptance that feelings such as anger are normal and acceptable.
- Encouraging the acceptance of responsibility for the behaviour that results from anger.

- Identification of the triggers, attitudes and beliefs that pre-dispose excessive anger.
- Identification of emotional baggage, e.g. fear, anxiety, denial, from the individual's background that reduces the likelihood of the correct expression of anger, and dealing with these issues.
- Development of an appropriate range of strategies to express anger.

Elaine Douglas suggests the **ASPIRE** response:

AS – Assess what is going on
P – Plan a response
I – Implement plan
R – Review
E – Evaluate success

This may involve encouraging individuals to think through their responses and consider if the situation could have been handled better, or in a way that resulted in a more positive outcome.

Training sessions require practice of scenarios so that the appropriate behaviours are rehearsed. For younger pupils, vocalizing their feelings and modelling responses can help to allow them to experiment with other alternative reactions. Vygotsky initially identified that many children control their behaviour by talking themselves through situations. Therefore encouraging pupils to sub-vocalize a phrase they have previously agreed and practised, e.g. '*I can walk away. I can walk away*', gradually replacing hot thoughts with cool thoughts and recognizing the physical signs in themselves that require action to avoid an outburst, can be helpful in changing initial and impulsive reactions to anger.

Other techniques that can be usefully explored include teaching relaxation techniques such as slow breathing, increased self-awareness of distraction techniques, avoidance of conflicting situations and assertiveness training, all of which can be instrumental in establishing ways of letting off steam that allow the child to remain in control.

Within school, consideration needs to be given to a teamwork response to anger and how this is modelled by the adults. A member of staff who him or herself models inappropriate responses to stress, e.g. irritability, or impulsive quick-tempered outbursts, is unlikely to encourage control in their pupils.

In the classroom, the most important aspect has to be to acknowledge the legitimacy of anger and recognize and praise positive responses to it. Planned ignoring of negative behaviours can be useful, as can increasing pupils' awareness of their own needs and the needs of others through story, drama and role-play.

With the individual child, the outcome must be focused upon:

- reducing the occurrence of anger through assessing the problem
- increasing motivation to retain control
- allowing opportunities for practice of these skills.

Care needs to be taken that areas that can exacerbate problems, such as learning difficulties, low self-esteem, and language difficulties, are addressed. Indicating a willingness to work through problems and finding a solution, followed up by praise for more successful outcomes, can allow pupils to manage their anger more effectively. Changes in behavioural responses will, however, take some time to establish.

8 Troubleshooting in Action: The Police and Schools

The information is this chapter is predominately the work of two currently serving police officers, Dr Andrew Briers and Paul Dunn. Both of these officers understand youth matters extremely well and provide many opportunities for multi-agency working to actually succeed in practice.

Safer Schools Community

The Behaviour Management page on the DfES website on 19 December 2005 stated the following with regards to behaviour in UK schools:

> It is hard to overestimate the damage a seriously disrupted education can do to a child's life chances. From the low-level backchat in the classroom to playground violence, bad behaviour affects the whole school community.

While commentators argue who is to blame – from parents to political correctness to TV violence – everyone agrees that we need to see a step-change in school discipline.

How bad is the problem and has it got worse?

As mentioned previously, there is a general perception that school discipline is out of control. While there is clearly a problem in a minority of schools, most children behave well, most of the time. While the number of *permanent exclusions* rose slightly in 2004/05, it has fallen by 20 per cent overall since 1997.

Ofsted's *Annual Report* found that behaviour was satisfactory or better in 99 per cent of primary and 94 per cent of secondary schools in the year 2004/05 – up from 91 per cent in 2003/04.

In terms of violence, in the one term for which we have detailed information, just 23 in 10,000 pupils were excluded for a fixed period for minor acts of violence.

Critics argue that teachers are powerless to deal with bad behaviour, bound by restrictive rules and at the mercy of appeals panels who can reinstate even the worst offenders, but if pupils have seriously broken school rules, or if their presence at school would harm other children or disrupt learning, the head-teacher may decide to exclude them, either for a fixed time or permanently.

As a result, a number of initiatives have taken place, including Safer Schools Partnerships, which involves dedicated police officers attached to primary and secondary schools that have high levels of offending and school exclusions. In addition, the option of voluntary Parenting Contracts, between a parent and a school, have already helped 2,000 parents improve their child's school attendance, with an extra 3,000 pupils attending secondary schools each day, every day. In this chapter we consider the option of the Safer Schools Partnership in some detail and an example of another type of voluntary Parent Contract currently in operation called an Acceptable Behaviour Contract, or ABC.

Safer Schools Partnerships

Studies carried out by MORI for the Youth Justice Board (2001) found that one in four school pupils across the country state that they have committed a crime and that one in five has armed him or herself. A staggering 23 per cent of excluded pupils state that they have been in possession of a gun and 44 per cent state that they have carried a knife.

In addition, what has been of concern to many teachers, school support workers and police liaison officers is that there are a significant number of crimes that are committed by children on the way to school, at school and again on the way home from school. Such children who inevitably become the repeat victims of these crimes are not surprisingly too scared to report these incidents for fear of retaliation from the perpetrators. These incidents are real and occur on a regular basis and the suspects and victims are all too aware of the rules that apply to the street, of which school is merely an extension.

There are many agencies that are working both singularly and in partnership to try to stem the numbers of young people who are finding themselves caught up in the criminal justice process and inevitably incarcerated in one of the country's young offender institutions. Some schemes have proved more successful than others at tackling youth crime from both a proactive and reactive role.

The Youth Justice Board in 2001 conducted a report to look at the risk and protective factors that lead to youth crime and any effective interventions to prevent it. The report highlighted risk and protective factors for youth crime into four main areas: the family, school, community and those, that are individual, personal and related to peer-group experiences.

Risk factors

Family risk factors include: poor parental supervision and discipline, family conflict, a family history of criminal activity, parental attitudes that condone anti-social behaviour, low income, poor housing and a large family size.

Risk factors in the school context include: low achievement beginning in primary school, aggressive behaviour (including bullying), lack of commitment to school (including truancy), and school disorganization, all of which increase the likelihood that young people exposed to them will become involved in crime.

Within the community, the risk factors identified by research are: living in a disadvantaged neighbourhood, community disorganization and neglect, availability of drugs and high turnover and lack of neighbourhood attachment.

Risk factors for youth crime that are essentially individual include: hyperactivity and impulsivity, low intelligence and cognitive impairment, alienation and lack of social commitment, attitudes that condone offending and drug misuse, and early involvement in crime and drug misuse. Friendships with peers involved in crime and drug misuse also increase the risk.

Protective factors

Factors that will protect against involvement in youth crime, even in the presence of the risk factors listed above, include: female gender, a resilient temperament, a sense of self-efficacy, a positive, outgoing disposition and high intelligence. Social bonding, and the promotion within the family, school and community of healthy standards will also act as protective factors.

Youth Justice Board November 2001

It therefore becomes apparent that to help protect children from these risks, parents, teachers and the community in general have a collective responsibility to lead by example and set out clear guidelines of how children should behave. School is naturally one arena which can significantly influence the lives of children and help shape and develop their lives and act as a means of protection against the associated risk factors:

Schools have the potential as a locus for crime prevention. They provide regular access to students throughout the developmental years, and perhaps the only consistent access to large numbers of the most crime-prone young children in the early school years; they are staffed with individuals paid to help youth develop as healthy, happy, productive citizens; and the community usually supports schools' efforts to socialize youth. Many of the precursors of delinquent behaviour are school-related and therefore likely to be amenable to change through school-based intervention.

Denise C. Gottfredson (1998)

There are currently a number of initiatives being adopted by the Government to combat children behaving badly at school and funding has been made available to target key areas such as truancy, exclusions and bad behaviour. The strategy is to support teachers by spotting problems early and intervening before truancy and exclusion is established in a school. This will be achieved in a variety of ways, including advice from specialists and additional training for teachers as part of their professional development.

A summary of measures that are currently used to reduce youth crime include BEST teams (Behaviour and Education Support Teams); parenting orders; youth inclusion programmes; education, training and employment programmes; and intensive supervision and surveillance programmes.

However, one additional area of support in UK schools has been the introduction of police officers in schools who are permanently attached either to an identified secondary school with a cluster of primary schools or some combination of arrangements, perhaps with a cohort of local schools. This differs markedly from other forms of intervention in that its purpose is to tackle crime and bad behaviour in schools in a proactive way, while offering support for teachers and victims. It is the emergence of two cultures, the police on the one hand and the teaching profession on the other, whose cultures, beliefs and values are markedly different.

The architect of the programme, Dr Andrew Briers, a former teacher and currently serving police officer, saw three main issues that needed to be addressed.

1   To develop trust and enhance relationships between school, the police and the community.
2   To represent the police in the community.
3   To develop and implement partnership activities with the local school to reduce crime and disorder in the area.

A list of the responsibilities and aims of the programme was developed in order to fulfil the goals of the project (see Figure 8.1).

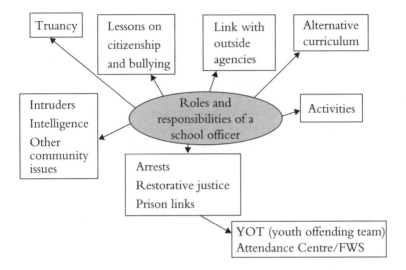

Safer School Communities (Briers 2004)

Figure. 8.1.   Responsibilities of a School Officer

Further, a list of aims were developed which are shown below.

To reduce the prevalence of crime and victimization among young people and to reduce the number of incidents and crimes in schools and their wider communities by:
–   working together to provide consistent and appropriate support and intervention to divert young people from social exclusion and criminality
–   sharing information to identify those young people at risk of becoming victims or offenders as well as those who already are.

To provide a safe and secure school community which enhances the learning environment by:
–   reducing the incidence of bullying and violent behaviour experienced by pupils and staff in school and the wider community
–   reducing substance misuse in the school and wider community
–   developing crime prevention strategies to improve the physical security of the school and the personal safety of all who use it

>   – developing a multi-agency approach to supporting teachers and other school staff in managing the learning environment.
>
> **To ensure that young people remain in education, actively learning and achieving their full potential by:**
>
>   – developing strategies to improve attendance by addressing both authorized and unauthorized absences
>
>   – supporting vulnerable young people through transition, between phases in their education and other aspects of their lives
>
>   – raising attainment by ensuring a calm learning environment free from disruption.
>
> **To engage young people, challenge unacceptable behaviour, and help them develop a respect for themselves and their community by:**
>
>   – developing a whole-school approach to conflict resolution
>
>   – ensuring that young people have opportunities to learn and develop citizenship skills
>
>   – promoting the full participation of all young people in the life of the school and its wider community and decisions that directly affect them.
>
> Safer School Partnership 2002

Establishing Roles and Responsibilities

From here the mechanics would need to be set up, which would involve all parties who have a vested interest in the scheme (parents, pupils, teachers, police, support staff, local community and school governors). A specific protocol for action should be written up by the school headteacher and seniorp police officer of the area, as well as the school beat officer who will ultimately have to undertake the role. Contained within this agreement will be issues such as:

- Aims and objectives
- The assignment of the school-based officer
- Hours of the school-based officer

- Safety
- Chain of command of the officer
- Training of the officer
- Dress code of the officer

Uniform of Police Officers
This is one key issue that has caused a great deal of debate. Although there are times when a flexible approach is necessary, the role of a schools officer is a uniformed one and requires the officer to be suitably dressed. The uniform is an effective tool for the officer and for many people this is still a form of authority which represents the police service and acts as a visible deterrent to intruders and a source of security and comfort.

Safety
Health and safety issues need to be considered regarding officers' use of equipment and facilities when carrying all their role within the school. Equipment should be stored safely when not in use and arrangement must ensure that no equipment is mislaid or able to be acquired by inquisitive children.

Chain of command
Clear guidelines regarding the chain of command will allow the officer to have a clear understanding of who is responsible for what, who to approach when they have concerns or questions and ultimately who is responsible and accountable for which areas. Examples of this would be the reporting of crime, what will be investigated, what are the hours of duty, and the job description.

Reporting of crime and arrests
What will constitute a crime in a school and who will deal with the matter? Is a playground fight a matter for police to deal with and treat as a crime, or is it a discipline matter for the school to take care of? Is there room for both to intervene, or will this cause friction within the partnership? Can officers arrest on site? Do they need the permission of the head, or can they use their discretion? There are a number of key issues here and work is currently under way to provide clear guidance on these

matters from the Youth Justice Board, who have consulted with the DfES and the Home Office to publish some standard form of reporting crime, and the way it should be dealt with, that provides a consistent message for schools and the police to work towards.

As with all these issues, it is for each individual school and the police to reach an agreement over the way the officer will work. Such a protocol should, where possible, be the same for each school in the area, so that officers who are called to deal with disturbances in their neighbouring school have an understanding of how they should operate. (The above two paragraphs are based on *Crime Recording by Police Officers Working in Schools* (Draft Youth Justice Board 2003.)

Communication with the headteacher
This cannot be emphasized enough, as the relationship developed between the officer and the head is often the mainstay of the partnership. Without the support and goodwill of the head, the scheme will experience extreme difficulties that will manifest themselves in a number of ways. To avoid this, officers need to meet regularly with their headteachers or the senior management team to update each other about what has been happening. This will enable the partnership to progress. Over time, relationships will develop, along with mutual trust, which will lead to a better understanding of each other's role and widen the scope for partnership working.

It is in these meetings that officers often become aware of the real issues that lay beneath the surface, in particular, the extent of crime that has been reported to the head or the levels of truancy and exclusion. For many officers the reluctance of heads to report crime is often a major cause of frustration and a stumbling block for the partnership. Heads are understandably reluctant to report all crimes to the police as the latter have a duty to report and investigate them. However, the deliberate cover-up of some serious incidents is contrary to the aim of the partnership and in light of this officers need to be able to fall back upon the agreed protocol and highlight the need for such crimes to be reported.

Selecting officers

Despite all the planning, the success of this programme ultimately lies in the qualities of the officer involved. Andrew Briers conducted a survey of teachers in 2002 which highlighted a number of qualities that teachers felt officers should possess in order to work in schools. They included a number of attributes, with a real concern and love for children being very much to the fore. The attributes were:

Ability to work in a team	Intelligent
Assertive	Personable
Calm	Personality and presence
Caring	Polite
Concerned	Professional at all times
Consistent	Respectful
Cooperative	Self-control
Discrete	Sensitive
Excellent counselling skills	Strict
Empathetic	Supportive
Good interpersonal skills	Sympathetic-looking
Integrity	Tactful

Based on these attributes, a job description and person specification for safer schools officers was published by the Safer Schools Partnership (2002). These are, however, a guide, and variations can be made to reflect a schools officer post in a particular area. (Specific details can be found in Briers 2004.)

Role of the officer

What did emerge fairly quickly was that there would be a specific need to provide some clear direction for the role of school officers within the framework of the Safer Schools Partnership (SSP) and local police force youth strategy incorporating the aims and objectives contained within. This was seen as best achieved by providing *all* officers with a modular programme of training, which covers the following four roles and ties in with the national policing model:

- Law
- Educator
- Adviser
- Role model

THE FOUR ROLES

Law – This role provides officers with a body of knowledge and understanding of the laws relating to dealing with pupils on school premises and how to carry out their duties in response to incidents of crime and anti-social behaviour. Key issues include powers of search, powers of arrest, educational laws, identification procedures, and the use of acceptable behaviour contracts.

Education – This role is split into two. First, there are educational inputs for pupils in the classroom setting around the key areas of citizenship. These might include visits to prisons or advice and information on safer routes to school for the pupils. The second strand concentrates on educating the officers and their educational colleagues in areas of child protection, critical incident training, officer safety and forensic opportunities, as well as how to deal with disruptive pupils and some of the reasons which trigger such behaviours.

Adviser – This role focuses on the officer acting in an advisory role to the pupils when dealing with some of the issues they face as part of a school community as well as for members of the staff. There is also a very important role to undertake with partnership agencies such as youth offending teams (YOTs), and Connexions, along with other colleagues and professionals within the police service and wider youth justice field.

Role model – This is a role that should not be overlooked as it plays an important part in building relationships between the police and young people. It helps young people to become better citizens and participate fully in school life and the wider community.

These four roles provide the basis for a job description for SSP officers. From closer examination of each role it becomes apparent where each role fits within the six strands of the Youth Strategy, which form the National Policing Plan.

The success of this programme in UK schools is being measured and audited as we speak but a remark by a fairly disaffected teenager in a North London to an SSP officer shows how the relationship between some communities and the police is being bridged: 'Me and my Dad always hated Old Bill but you . . . you're all right.'

Voluntary Multi-Agency Contracts

One of the benefits that closer cooperation between schools and external agencies can generate is new ideas about how to manage similar problems but in different environments. An example of this is the use of school Acceptable Behaviour Contracts, or ABCs, which were originally used between housing associations, youths and families involved in anti-social behaviour. An ABC is a written agreement/contract between a person who has been involved in unacceptable behaviour and one or more local agencies whose role it is to prevent such behaviour.

The contract specifies a list of anti-social acts which the person has committed and which they agree not to continue committing. Where possible the individual should be involved in drawing up the contract. This may encourage them to recognize the impact their behaviour has and to take responsibility for their actions. Support to address the underlying causes of the behaviour should be offered in parallel with the contract. This may include diversionary activities (such as attendance at a youth project), counselling or support for the family. It is vital to ascertain which agencies are already involved, especially where the individual is aged between 10 and 17 years.

Paul Dunn, a serving Police Officer in the Metropolitan Police who originally designed the contract, states that:

> ABCs are an opportunity to involve an individual or group of individuals and those responsible for their behaviour in a discussion about the meaning of the term 'anti-social behaviour' and the impact on others. They should be used as part of an early intervention to stop the bad behaviour and to warn the perpetrator or/and family of possible repercussions should the behaviour continue. In addition, it is an opportunity to provide positive solutions to address serious issues such as family problems, which may be identified before, during and after the course of the meeting.

The contract was designed initially for 10 to 18-year-olds, but this can be flexible. In the case of under 10s, the parent(s)/carer(s) sign a Parental Control Agreement, or PCA. This is the same as an ABC except that the parent(s)/carer(s) take full responsibility for their child's behaviour. The child would not be asked to sign the contract.

Although an ABC is not legally binding, a breached ABC would show that the individual will not voluntarily change their behaviour and therefore can be used in the context of more formalized proceedings within the school discipline code or perhaps within the courts.

All parties must be present at the interview to enable full discussion and the drawing up and signing of the contract; this will include the parent(s)/carer(s), school representatives, the SSP officer and any other interested party such as a social worker, family members or supportive friends. There have been occasions when the family has brought along a solicitor.

The contract normally lasts for six months although it can be renewed after a case conference has been held. This runs in conjunction with the evidence-gathering period of an ASBO. The time limit can be flexible as long as it is fair and proportionate to the issues raised. School ABCs have greater flexibility and can range from a matter of weeks to a school term or year.

It has been proved over an extended period of time now that individuals who participate in the scheme have had previous and sometimes numerous dealings with various agencies, usually working in isolation of each other. Especially in the case of young people, ABCs allow more proactive interventions at an early stage, actually dealing with the issues before they develop into major concerns.

An example of an ABC is given here, but it must be remembered that flexibility is essential in both the mechanics of drawing up a contract and the conditions of application.

Acceptable Behaviour Contract

Students and staff at this school are committed to maintaining a safe school community, free from abuse, distress and violence. The police and local authority are working with the school where necessary to help with this. Where students have presented a serious breach of the school's Code for Learning and have demonstrated behaviour that challenges the safety of the school community and its positive learning environment, they place themselves at serious risk of exclusion from the school. As a part of their Pastoral Support Plan, which is designed to help the student make the positive choices necessary to stay at this school, an Acceptable Behaviour Contract is agreed between the student, school, parents/carers and the police.

This contract is made on (date) ....…...….......…............ ....

Between............…......…......... ... .…................

And (name)..........….............. ....…. ....

Date of birth ….…...............… .. ..…...................….................

Address   ....

....

I (name) .... agree the following regarding my future behaviour.

---

1. I will not
2. I will not
3. I will
4. I will
5. I will

I understand that if I do anything which breaks the terms of this contract the school may take further action against me.

Student.............................. Print name..............….................

Parent/Carer...................…........ Print name ....…......

School representative........... Print name ....….......

Police officer.......…................ Print name ....…......

Review date...

9 Troubleshooting in Action: The Role of Alternative Treatment Options

Alternative treatments and complementary therapies are available to assist with a range of learning difficulties and behavioural issues and have been growing in popularity. Although no 'magic bullet' exists, options can be tried which work in conjunction with traditional strategies for managing learning and behavioural issues. In this chapter I discuss a series of alternative treatments and provide links to relevant external websites where additional information can be found.

Therapies

There are a wide variety of alternative therapies currently available for children experiencing learning difficulties, ranging from speech to music or even exercise-based therapy. Some of the most common are dealt with below.

Speech and Language Therapy

Speech and language therapists (SLTs)are specialists in communication disorders and can be of great help to people experiencing a range of needs from mild to severe learning difficulties, dyslexia, dysfluency and autism. SLTs work to assess, diagnose and develop a programme of care to maximize the communication potential of the people referred to them. To help an individual to function to the best of their ability, an SLT may work directly with a person with communication difficulties but will also be involved in breaking down communication barriers by influencing and supporting those in the person's communication environment.

The following websites provide detailed information and contacts for accredited therapists.

- The Royal College of Speech and Language Therapists, www.rcslt.org
- The Association of Speech and Language Therapists in Independent Practice, www.asltip.co.uk

Music Therapy

Music therapy is a creative, non-verbal tool which is increasingly recognized as a valuable part of the care of people who have sensory, physical, learning or neurological disabilities, or who have emotional or behavioural problems. The therapy is the development of a *relationship* between the client and therapist and music-making forms the basis for communication in this relationship.

Music can be used to promote developmental work. Involvement in creative music-making can assist physical awareness and develop attention, memory and concentration. It can also provide a safe setting where difficult or repressed feelings may be expressed and contained. By offering support and acceptance the therapist can help the person to work towards emotional release and self-acceptance.

The following further information on music therapy and practitioners:

- www.apmt.org
- www.bsmt.org

Exercise Therapy

Both the British Dyslexia Association and the Dyslexia Institute want more research to be carried out into the use of exercise programmes following a study in a primary school in the Midlands that said it had seen remarkable improvement in pupils with dyslexia who had taken in the new exercise programme, the Dyslexia, Dyspraxia and Attention disorder Treatment (DDAT). DDAT offers a highly structured exercise-based treatment designed to address the root cause of the cerebellar developmental delay condition (CDD), the area of the brain responsible for motor skills and processing. Having assessed the extent of the problem using eye, balance and cognitive skills tests, an individual exercise programme is prescribed to improve cerebellar function, resulting in improvements in motor skill learning and the ability to learn new skills rather than an improvement in practised skills alone.

For further information on the DDAT programme or DDAT centres (located in Kenilworth, London, Bedford, Sheffield, Edinburgh, Manchester, Cardiff and Southampton) telephone DDAT on 0870 880 8791 (8.00–5.30 Monday to Friday). Other organizations are:

- The Dore Programme, www.ddat.co.uk
- The Dyslexia Institute, www.dyslexia-inst.org.uk

Information and Communication Technology (ICT)

ICT is a growing area in which children experiencing emotional and behavioural difficulties can find a non-threatening environment in which to achieve success. For many, learning may have become associated with fear of failure, both in their own eyes and in the eyes of those around them. The computer can provide a neutral setting in which to experiment, with students confident that they are controlling the pace and level of work. Many learners with EBD find it hard to establish relationships, and have little ability or perceived need to relate to others. Using a computer can avoid this problem and can often offer an entry point for another person to join in alongside in a non-threatening manner.

A variety of ICT equipment can also help students with learning difficulties. Devices such as handheld spellcheckers and calculators can support learners who have difficulties with sequencing and memorizing. Multimedia technology, which can present sounds, photographs and video, as well as text and graphics on the screen, gives new directions for working with all students who have learning difficulties. The ability to take a photograph and immediately display it on the computer screen with a recorded message presents opportunities for learning which are not so dependent on the written word.

- For a more in-depth discussion on this topic consult www. ictadvice.org.uk

Nutrition and Supplements

A good diet is important for good health. According to the British Nutrition Foundation, a healthy diet is based on breads, potatoes, and other cereals and is rich in fruits and vegetables. A healthy diet will include moderate amounts of milk and dairy products, meat, fish or meat/milk alternatives, and limited amounts of foods containing fat or sugar.

No single food can provide all the essential nutrients that the body needs. Therefore, it is important to consume a wide variety of foods to provide adequate intakes of vitamins, minerals and dietary fibre, which are important for health. It is also important to remember that dietary requirements change as we grow and can be different for men and women from an early age. For a detailed analysis of a lifetime's nutritional requirements consult the British Nutrition Foundation website.

Diet is important not only for physical health but also for optimal mental development and functioning. Nutrition can affect everyday difficulties in behaviour, learning or mood that can affect children and adults at home, at school or in the workplace including developmental conditions, such as ADHD, dyslexia, dyspraxia, autistic spectrum disorders, and mental health conditions, such as anxiety, depression, bipolar (manic-depressive) disorder and schizophrenia.

As the *Guardian* reported (2 May 2005), new studies show British children are suffering from behavioural and learning disorders because their diets are deficient in vital nutrients needed for their brain to function normally. Much of the research conducted into the relationship between nutrition and learning difficulties centres on deficiencies in fatty acids. Dr Alex Richardson, Senior Research Fellow at Mansfield College and University Laboratory of Physiology, Oxford University, reports:

Scientific evidence suggests that imbalances or deficiencies of certain highly unsaturated fatty acids (HUFA) may contribute to a range of behavioural and learning difficulties including ADHD, dyslexia, dyspraxia, and autistic spectrum disorders.

These omega-3 and omega-6 fatty acids are found in fish and seafood, some nuts and seeds and green leafy vegetables. They are absolutely essential for normal brain development and function, but are often lacking from modern diets. Everyone needs adequate dietary supplies of these HUFA for mental and physical health, but research shows that some people may need higher levels in their diet than others. Constitutional individual differences in metabolism that would increase dietary requirements include:

- difficulties in the conversion of simple essential fatty acids (EFA) into the more complex HUFA that the brain needs, i.e. DGLA and AA (omega-6), and EPA and DHA (omega-3)
- unusually rapid breakdown and loss of these HUFA
- difficulties in recycling, transporting or incorporating HUFA into cell membranes.

There is some evidence for each of these factors in ADHD, dyslexia, dyspraxia, and autism.

Food supplements of HUFA may therefore help in the management of these conditions. Controlled trials have provided preliminary evidence for this in ADHD and dyslexia, but further treatment trials are still needed, especially with respect to dyspraxia (now under way) and autism.

Research indicates that omega-3 fatty acids are more likely to help than omega-6 (although both are important for optimal brain function). Of the omega-3 fatty acids, the latest evidence indicates that it is EPA – not DHA – that is likely to be most beneficial for these purposes.

It is essential to recognize that ADHD, dyslexia, dyspraxia, or autistic spectrum disorders are simply descriptive labels for particular patterns of behavioural and learning difficulties. In practice, the individual differences between people with any of these labels are substantial, and most show features of more than one of these conditions. Furthermore, fatty acid deficiency is clearly only one possible contributory factor. There are many potential causes of behavioural and learning difficulties, and for any individual all such avenues should be investigated. For these reasons fatty acid supplements cannot be expected to help in every case, but potential indicators of a good response to this approach include:

- physical signs of fatty acid deficiency (excessive thirst, frequent urination, rough or dry 'bumpy' skin, dry, dull or 'lifeless' hair, dandruff, and soft or brittle nails)
- allergic tendencies (such as eczema, asthma, hayfever, etc.)
- visual symptoms (such as poor night vision, sensitivity to bright light, or visual disturbances when reading, e.g. letters and words may appear to move, swim or blur on the page)
- attentional problems (distractibility, poor concentration and difficulties in working memory)
- emotional sensitivity (such as depression, excessive mood swings or undue anxiety)
- sleep problems (especially difficulties in settling at night and waking in the morning).

Ongoing research will help to clarify the importance of these features as indicators of relative HUFA deficiency. Although common in dyslexia, dyspraxia, ADHD and autistic spectrum disorders, they are certainly not confined to individuals with these conditions.

About 5 per cent of children with ADHD respond to particular substances in their diet in a direct and obvious way. However, healthy eating, with regular varied food, which provides a constant blood sugar level through out the day, will be beneficial for all pupils. Children from a chaotic home where one or other parent may also have a degree of ADHD may well not be provided with a particularly nourishing lunchbox. It can be an ongoing challenge.

The thinking on Coke or Red Bull intake is variable. There are some young children who respond in a very active way to the caffeine or the sugar load in these drinks. However, drug companies in the USA have investigated using caffeine as a treatment but found that the efficacy was limited by side-effects such as the shakes, and loss of appetite.

Fish oils

Efalex is an over-the-counter dietary supplement containing fish oils which is marketed 'to improve brain function'. In the USA it has been marketed to treat ADHD but at present this marketing campaign has had to be withdrawn due to inconclusive evidence. There are a number of ongoing studies. The balanced view appears to be that it may provide some improvement in brain functioning but not to the same degree as established treatments such as stimulants. When given with stimulants there may be an additive effect of making fits more likely in a susceptible child. EyeQ is a similar supplement.

For further news articles on fatty acids and vitamins see:

- www.dyslexichelp.co.uk   Home>Site   index>alternative approaches to dyslexia>Nutrition
- www.nas.org.uk Home>How to get help>Information sheets>Approaches, therapies, interventions>Diets and Vitamins.
- www.nutrition.org.uk

Several companies, some of which are listed below, specialize in high quality supplements:

- Efamol: www.efamol.com Home>Health Guide
- 1st Vitality: www.1stvitality.com Home>A-Z of Health

Nutritional assessments are a good way to comprehensively discover if the nutritional needs of your child are being met. These tests should be conducted by a qualified nutritional therapist or dietician, who can be located via the following websites:

- www.nutritionsociety.org.uk/membership/register/
- www.dietitiansunlimited.co.uk

Medication

Medication in school can provide considerable benefits and challenges. Details of the common medications used are provided below. If you would like additional information on a particular medication, your local pharmacy can provide further product specification details.

Stimulant medication allows the child to concentrate and pay attention. It is not given to children because they are sick, but rather to improve the way their brain functions. Stimulants work by changing the levels of brain chemicals and making receptors in the brain work more efficiently. This makes focusing as well as learning easier. They can also help decrease impulsivity.

Methylphenidate is by far the most common drug used for medical intervention. It has a controlled drug status, where prescriptions have to be written in a certain way and parents are therefore advised to plan ahead carefully for repeat prescriptions to avoid delays. It comes in short, intermediate, and long acting pills.

Ritalin and Equasym are the brand names for the short acting methylphenidate. This medication usually starts working in about 20 minutes. Its effects last for about four hours. Ritalin was first commercially released for use in 1957. There is extensive research indicating short-term effectiveness: 70 to 80 per cent of children with ADHD find it useful. There is no evidence that it leads to dependency.

The intermediate release versions of methylphenidate include Ritalin slow-release. This tablet lasts up to six hours but has not proved to be very predictable in its effects and is therefore not often used.

There are two long acting versions called Concerta XL, which works for 12 hours, and Equasym XL, which works for six to eight hours. A disadvantage of these preparations is that they may cause more concern at school because staff may not be aware if medication has been discontinued or the dosage changed.

As these medicines are stimulants they can be abused. At the present time Ritalin appears to have a street value of about 80p per tablet. Because Concerta is absorbed more slowly it does not have the same street value. There may be issues about travelling abroad with a child on methylphenidate due to customs regulations. It is therefore usually suggested that a covering letter from the GP is also taken.

There is considerable debate about whether a child who performs well in the sporting arena should be allowed to take methylphenidate. The relevant national sporting organizations are happy to give advice regarding this.

There are some occupational considerations. For example, the Ministry of Defence will not consider employing anyone who has been on stimulant medication over the previous two years.

Dexamfetamine acts in a very similar way to methylphenidate. 'Dexedrine' is the brand name for dexamfetamine. The effects of dexamfetamine last for about four hours. It is usually used as a second-line treatment when a trial with methylphenidate has failed. It is also available in the USA as a long-acting version called Adderal XR. This would only be available on special request in this country.

Action of stimulants

Both methylphenidate and dexamfetamine have a direct effect on attention, short-term memory, vigilance, reaction time, listening skills and on-task behaviours. Tests on driving abilities show a clear improvement for those on stimulant medication. They do not treat associated problems such as oppositional and anti-social behaviours, learning difficulties or emotional immaturity. However, as they improve concentration, they may have an indirect beneficial effect on some of these behaviours. They are not a cure for ADHD and apart from Concerta and Adderal XR are very short acting in the body. When they are no longer in the bloodstream, the ADHD symptoms return. They enable ADHD children to reach their full potential and work towards long-term goals. The child can then get the most from interventions such as special education programmes, or social skills training.

Common side-effects

These include loss of appetite, nervousness, crying, irritability, sleep problems, headaches, and stomachaches. Most of these side-effects improve after about a week. A rash may occasionally occur and parents are advised to stop medication if this does not settle within a few days. If there are rebound effects such as an increased level of activity and impulsivity beyond that normally experienced by the untreated child the dosage may need further adjustment.

This drug can help with attention and concentration difficulties and behavioural problems. It is the first-line treatment for tics. It can be used alone or in combination with stimulants. It can be particularly useful for sleep problems and aggressive outbursts. It stimulates the alpha 2 adrenergic receptors in the central nervous system. It is usually given as a tablet. Dixarit tablets are blue and are 25 micrograms in size. There are also some generic tablets, which are white and are also 25 micrograms. The dose is 3 to 5 micrograms per kilo of body weight. It is usually given in divided doses four times a day. It has its highest concentration in the body five hours after taking the tablets. The effect lasts for six to eight hours. It may take up to one month for the highest benefits.

Side-effects include some patients feeling sleepy to start with or when there is an increase in the drug dosage. They may also notice a dry mouth. Occasionally there are problems with dizziness or feelings of faintness. This is unusual at low doses. There are no withdrawal symptoms if you stop the medication gradually. If the medication is stopped suddenly there may be a rise in blood pressure, restlessness, difficulty sleeping, headaches, sweating, muscle pains and abdominal pains.

Risperidone is in a class of drugs known as 'atypical antipsychotics' which were first developed to treat psychosis. It has been used in adults for about fifteen years. More recently there have been a number of studies that suggest it may be effective for children on the autistic spectrum to help with their poor tolerance to frustration. Parents and children have both reported considerable benefits. There are a few small-scale studies suggesting that it might be used for children with ADHD who get impulsively angry. It is often used when home or school situations may be about to break down irreparably. Results can be dramatic.

Compared to the older antipsychotics, risperidone is relatively side-effect free. The most common side effects include weight gain and drowsiness. In the very long term (20 years of use) it may cause abnormal movements which are irreversible. As these pills have not yet been used for this long in young people their effect on the developing brain is unknown. In the short term, unusually, a young person may respond to an initial dose with muscle rigidity. Extremely rarely there is a risk of malignant neuroleptic syndrome with muscle stiffness, and very high temperature. This is a medical emergency and requires immediate treatment. This can happen at any stage of treatment and is not dose related.

Melatonin is sometimes prescribed to help children with ADHD settle to sleep. It makes one sleepy for about two hours and has no hangover effect the following morning. It will not help with early morning wakening or if you wake in the middle of the night. It is a synthetic version of a natural hormone. It is not licensed as a medicine in the UK. Locally it requires two consultant signatures to initiate prescribing and further prescriptions have to be obtained from the hospital. There have been no regularly noted side-effects.

Atomoxetine is a new drug and is sold under the trade name of Strattera which is being used in the USA and was given a licence here in June 2004. The trials have been very encouraging. As well as working on concentration it has a slight anti-anxiety effect. It is a once-daily medication which works in the prefrontal cortex to increase the availability of noradrenaline. Unlike the stimulants, it needs to be given regularly and the maximum benefit is noted after four weeks of constant administration. Drug holidays are therefore not recommended. It covers both the early mornings and the evenings so that it has a positive effect on family life. Unlike stimulants, it is not a 'controlled drug' and in theory therefore has no risk of abuse.

It can have an effect on appetite which improves on taking the drug regularly. It may also cause headaches, vomiting and dizziness. These again may improve over time. It has only been prescribed widely since 2003, so there needs to be some caution about long-term effects.

Which Medication?

Drug	Trade name	Length of effect	Principle effect
Methylphenidate	Ritalin	4 hours	Improves concentration
	Equasym	4 hours	Improves concentration
	Ritalin slow release	8 hours	Improves concentration
	Equasym XL	6–8 hours	Improves concentration
	Concerta XL	12 hours	Improves concentration
Dexamfetamine	Dexedrine	4 hours	Improves concentration
	Adderal	8 hours	Improves concentration
Clonidine	Dixarit	4–6 hours	Improves impulsivity and angry outbursts
Risperidone	Risperdal	12 hours	Improves angry outbursts
Melatonin		2 hours	Helps to settle to sleep
Atomoxetine	Strattera	3 hours in bloodstream, 24 hour effect in the brain	Improves concentration and impulsivity

10 Troubleshooting in Action: Child Depression, Counselling and Coaching

In Chapter 6, when I talked about supporting and sustaining structure and flexibility I made the point that in order to establish the 3Rs (Respect, Relationships, Role models) the issue of relationships would often require specialist input: and it is to this area that I now turn. Before we do this, however, let us consider some of the reasons why this is such an important issue.

Although not all children with behavioural issues have low self-esteem, it is something that needs to be addressed in many cases. All children and young people experience highs and lows, particularly in adolescence when hormonal changes make confusion and anxiety more likely. However, in some children these low feelings dominate all areas of their life and develop into an illness that is not just an adult condition and results in depression.

Incidence

Some authorities consider that two out of 100 children under 12 are depressed to such an extent that they would benefit from psychiatric help, and four or five out of 100 show signs of significant distress. The incidence increases with age and is higher in inner-city areas. In a primary school with 250 pupils, three children may be depressed and a further 11 suffering from significant levels of emotional distress. In a secondary school with 1,000 pupils the equivalent figures are clearly even higher, with up to 50 being depressed and 100 suffering serious distress. However, few pupils are formally diagnosed. This could be associated with the stigma attached to mental health but is perhaps also related to a perception that mental health issues are associated with adults.

Depression in children, if left untreated, can lead to academic underachievement, social isolation and create difficult relationships both within and outside school. It is also associated with an increased risk of suicide, which is the third leading cause of death for 15 to 24-year-olds and the sixth leading cause of death for 5-to-14 year olds. It has been estimated that more than 90 per cent of children and adolescents who take their own lives have a mental health disorder such as depression. Once a young person has experienced depression, they are five times more likely to have depression as an adult.

Causes

Depression in young people often occurs with other mental and physical illnesses such as anxiety and diabetes. There is no one cause for depression but there are risk factors that may make its occurrence more likely. The main factors are listed below, and it will come as no surprise that some of these have featured previously in this book:

- loss – separation of parents, loss of friendships, or bereavement
- high levels of stress – family problems, abuse, exam pressure, bullying or serious illness
- learning disorders
- disruptive behaviour
- family history of depression.

Both genders are at equal risk for developing depression, but during adolescence girls are twice as likely to exhibit symptoms as boys.

Depression in children can remain unrecognized by adults. This may be because children do not have the words to express how they are feeling and the symptoms may be seen as part of changes that take place during maturation. Sometimes the evident unhappiness may be attributed to other known factors and the physical complaints that can accompany depression may become the sole focus of attention.

Symptoms

The symptoms of depression in children and adolescents are the same as they are in adults. However, recognition and diagnosis may be more difficult in youth as the way symptoms are expressed varies with the developmental stage of the child. Some of symptoms that may be observed within school and could be associated with depression in children include:

- frequent complaints of vague, non-specific physical ailments such as headaches, muscle aches, stomachaches or tiredness
- frequent absences from school or poor performance in school
- talk of or efforts to run away from school and/or home
- outbursts of shouting, complaining, irritability or crying
- low tolerance of frustration
- lack of interest in previous activities or hobbies
- complaining of being bored but unable to focus or settle
- lack of interest in being with friends
- disruption in sleep and eating patterns
- social isolation and reluctance to communicate
- talk or fear of death
- extreme sensitivity to rejection or failure
- increased anger or hostility
- reckless behaviour
- extreme externalization or internalization of blame
- difficulty with relationships.

Treatment

Children and adolescents with depressive disorders can receive treatments such as antidepressant medication, short-term psychotherapy, counselling, creative therapies, or a combination of these treatments. In the UK, antidepressant medication is used rarely with children as there remains a lack of evidence on the benefit of this medication in children and adolescents. However, a review of studies involving 8 to 19-year-olds with moderate depression concluded that treatment that focused on how to change children's thinking and behaviour (Cognitive Behaviour Treatment) brought significant benefits. There is less evidence about the effectiveness of treatment with a focus on encouraging children to talk about their feelings (psychodynamic treatment) but research studies suggest that the majority improve if they have frequent sessions (Roth 1996).

Supporting Children with Depression in School

Depression is an illness and its diagnosis and treatment is not something that comes within the remit of schools. However, schools are able to take action that can target the risk factors and by undertaking such action might reduce both the incidence of depression and the impact it has on learning. Action, reflection and reaction could be taken to reduce anxiety and emotional stress that may result from:

- pupil disability
- sensory and physical impairments, illness, etc.
- skill development delays: learning difficulties, social problems, attention difficulties
- emotional difficulties
- low self-esteem
- stressful life events, family disorganization and conflict, and poor bonding to parents
- relationship problems
- peer rejection, alienation and isolation
- lack of success and school failure
- environmental risks such as community disharmony, racial tension and equality.

Supporting children diagnosed as exhibiting depression or suspected as having raised levels of anxiety is also important and needs to be planned for. Identification is often key to effective responses and is rarely straightforward as the affected pupils themselves are unlikely to realize that they are developing an illness. In addition they may feel unable to take action to help themselves. Therefore, increasing staff, parent and child awareness of the need to alert school support services when children's behaviours change, for example if they become withdrawn, their work suffers, they become angry without justifiable reason, appear unkempt and express views that suggest they see little of value in themselves or others, is important. The involvement of parents and external agencies, at the same time recognizing the issue of child confidentiality, should stem from previously decided and communicated information aimed at ensuring that appropriate agreed action is instigated.

Counselling in Schools

One area that can be utilized as an option for treating depression but has a great deal to offer many children with other behavioural issues is counselling. Counselling, as described by the British Association for Counselling and Psychotherapy (BACP), takes place when 'a person occupying regularly or temporarily the role of counsellor, offers and agrees explicitly to give time, attention and respect to another person'.

It would appear that changes in society have reduced the opportunities available to young people to have someone with whom to discuss, formalize and clarify their thinking, especially those students with behavioural difficulties. Providing these opportunities within school has been completed informally through initiatives such as Circle Time and PSHE discussion, but with the child who needs more personal and individual support this assistance can be patchy. The increased pressure in schools has meant that often teachers do not have time to implement individual responses and, many would argue, lack the specific training and skills to undertake this task.

Counselling is a process which assists the individual to focus upon their concerns while simultaneously exploring problems, making choices, managing crises and working through feelings of conflict. It allows children and young people to gain a better understanding of themselves and of situations, as well as to develop strategies to manage change.

Counselling in schools can provide a cost-effective service for pupils indicating emotional distress and/or behavioural problems, as a result of emotional stress arising from influences such as relationship difficulties, loss and anxiety. When emotional distress is not addressed, tension can build up leading to deterioration in a pupil's attitude and mental stamina. These difficulties can contribute to truancy, reduced school performance and disaffection.

Emotional well-being is clearly correlated with learning and it is not possible for schools to improve learning outcomes and provide for the inclusion of all children, without considering the impact of emotional stress on attainment.

The DfES describes counselling as an important element of support for children and young people with emotional and behavioural difficulties. In addition, in DfES guidance aimed at promoting positive mental health, counselling is recognized as an important early intervention and preventive strategy to reduce pupils' stress levels.

Ofsted, meanwhile, has consistently referred to counselling in schools as complementing pastoral care systems, supporting the management of children with emotional and behavioural difficulties, and supporting effective child protection procedures.

Which Children Benefit from Counselling?
Counselling is likely to benefit a pupil who:

- indicates a sudden drop in the standard of their work
- demonstrates extreme mood swings
- shows indicators of school refusal
- bullies or is bullied
- may have experienced abuse
- has experienced loss
- indicates emotional responses to stress, e.g. self-harming, eating disorders, etc.

What Is the Purpose of Counselling and Who Provides It?
The purpose of counselling is to support pupils sufficiently to allow them to function effectively, access the curriculum and engage with the activities offered within school. It is important, however, to make the distinction between the informal counselling skills used by staff in schools, and the process of counselling

used by trained and qualified counsellors. As issues that arise can be highly sensitive it is important to use trained and accountable practitioners as counsellors in schools.

There will obviously be a great difference for practising counsellors between working in a clinical setting and in a school, therefore intervention needs to be adapted to fit the circumstances. For instance, there may be pressure upon counsellors to see troubled youngsters quickly and to provide support that has an immediate impact.

However effective it would be in theory, it would be difficult in practice to combine the role of counsellor with that of teacher as the two roles may conflict; for example, discipline and liaison with parents, and the necessity to establish equality of status between counsellor and client, could lead to problems in combining roles. Therefore most schools employ qualified counsellors, although there may remain conflict relating to confidentiality and parental permission/right to know.

Counselling can take a number of forms but increasingly popular is Brief Counselling, as it fits in with the time constraints of school-based intervention and is aimed at giving the child a 'quick fix' rather than the deeper processes of reconstruction that is the focus of psychodynamic therapy.

Though research has shown that in some cases two or three sessions can lead to improvements for particular pupils, if the aim has been to change both behaviour and emotional responses then a number of sessions will be required.

Finding the right type of person to provide the service is not easy as often both children and staff will be somewhat sceptical and suspicious of 'shrinks' and, in any case, it can be a difficult process for pupils who struggle to develop relationships. In addition, some of the other issues that will need to be addressed include:

- provision of an environment that allows pupils to feel secure enough to expose their feelings
- constraints of timetable
- counselling aims that are in keeping with the school ethos
- resources for counselling

- planning and sustaining counselling programmes
- counselling styles that respond to child needs
- identification of techniques that are appropriate in school.

Guidelines for Counselling in Schools, a free booklet produced from collaboration between BACP and the Gulbenkian Foundation, stated that 80 per cent of those receiving counselling were 'reporting significant improvements in their situations as a direct result. A majority also reported feeling better in themselves and as having gained in confidence and self-esteem.'

In practice, as it becomes obvious that the results of counselling are having a positive effect on changing the behaviour and attitude of specific children, it has been my experience that both children and staff understand its value to the school community.

The Boundaries for Counselling in School

Issues surrounding confidentiality and ethics need to clarified before schools progress down the counselling route. The situation is complex and made increasingly so by the ever-more legalistic climate. Matters relating to child protection are often a concern as the school is under a legal obligation to report these to Social Services, meaning that the counsellor will then have to break the confidentiality of the client. Concerns relating to the keeping of records, the possibility of suicide and inappropriate sexual conduct all place constraints upon counsellors working in school that may not apply in other settings. Indeed, it may be that if too many restrictions are placed upon the counsellor, the counselling itself becomes less effective. Also, it needs to be stated that the counselling approach may not be effective for everybody, as the style of both person and the approach taken is just not proactive for some individuals.

Coaching

For many, the terms mentoring and coaching appear to be interchangeable, but it is important to make a distinction between the two. Mentoring is usually considered to be an activity that takes place usually in a one-to-one situation with one person being the leader and the other the learner. In contrast, coaching is instead taken to be an equal partnership collaboration, that suggests working alongside an individual or a group in order to achieve shared aims. Coaching supports improvement in specific skill areas and is most effective when there is a clear agenda to address that is central to the performance of the individual at the school. Coaching can support individuals in schools by:

- developing knowledge and skills
- engendering trust and responsibility
- providing a supportive culture.

Why are coaching strategies useful in class?

The National Forum for Educational Research (NFER) has identified, following research, what they describe as the 'invisible children' – those with no obvious difficulties or strengths, but the often average-attaining child, who may drift through his or her education rather than actively participate in action to increase outcomes. In a school that facilitates a coaching approach, during each lesson the teachers and teaching assistants encourage verbal interaction and use this as a springboard to motivate pupils to contribute observations and explore further a particular aspect or topic. This facilitates discussion, provides clarity and moves learning on.

Coaching focuses on improving the learning outcomes for all by providing greater focus and awareness of choice. It concentrates on the stage each pupil has reached at that time and encourages shared responsibility to achieve where they want to be tomorrow. It targets the attainment of all children as it is centred around the skills necessary for future progress. Success requires changes in behaviour and so the adults within the school actively explore and promote a learning environment that encourages risk-taking behaviour, where incorrect responses are valued as much as correct ones for the value they give to comprehending the pupil's present level of understanding. Coaching provides environments where all individuals can partake in discussion and where arrangements for grouping ensure all feel able to participate and that their view is valued.

In brief, schools that observe and implement active coaching should aim for:

- increased learning skills
- the promotion of positive attitudes and outlooks through modelling
- espousing not just 'talking the talk but walking the walk' – providing planned opportunities to practise newly learned skills and experiences
- increased independence of children in locating ways forward and undertaking the action necessary to move ahead
- increased ability of all individuals to engage with learning
- consistent shared responsibility for peers to support the coaching of others.

The benefits for schools that use coaching techniques across the curriculum include:

- increased understanding and control of their own role in achieving success
- improved ability to communicate views and opinions
- enhanced abilities to make informed choices
- improved ability to see obstacles to success as challenges to be overcome
- improved emotional intelligence and the willingness to accept differing roles and accept other's ideas
- reduced anxiety and more risk-taking behaviour
- increased ability to become proactive in locating solutions to individual difficulties
- reduced risk of marginalization and self-isolation of pupils
- development of teamwork approaches to solving problems
- emphasis placed upon building relationships to encourage interaction and reflection upon learning experiences
- promotion of communication and understanding between all stakeholders
- development of a learning community.

Skills within staff that underpin coaching and need to be supported include:

- communication and interpersonal skills
- creative thinking
- active listening
- reflective and open questioning
- facilitating confidence in others and self to make mistakes and seeing these as learning opportunities
- promoting motivation to achieve aims
- being comfortable with ambiguity and disagreement.

Coaching techniques can only be successful if seen as part of a strategic intervention that aims to increase the success of all, rather than a way of supporting individual needs. It requires the support of the whole organization and may require a significant amount of preparation work to ensure that skills and attitudes are conducive to its application. Coaching requires trust and this suggests that relationships are paramount to its success. It also requires a considerable investment in time allocation to provide training, opportunities for reflection and implementation.

11 Troubleshooting in Action: Learning Behaviour and Working with Parents

In Chapter 1 it was mentioned that a special task force was established in the UK to consider behaviour and discipline and to give advice to the Government on how behaviour in schools could be improved. Their report, issued in October 2005, consisted of ten policy chapters and made 84 recommendations that covered areas such as: implementing existing policies; spreading good practice; training; diet; sport and the wider curriculum; exclusions and alternative provision; schools working in collaboration; support and guidance for parents; school building design; and new powers.

Many of the recommendations required Government action but those that required school action included the following:

- An audit of behaviour management, teaching and learning, school leadership, classroom management, rewards and sanctions, behaviour strategies, the teaching of good behaviour, staff development, pupil support systems, liaison with parents and other agencies, transition and facilities to assess impact on pupil behaviour.
- Regular use of self-evaluation tools for behaviour and attendance.
- Headteachers to reflect upon the interaction between learning, teaching and behaviour when completing the school self-evaluation form.
- Schools to adopt a proposed National Behaviour Charter.
- Schools to have policies on the use of mobile phones.
- Schools to identify a member of the leadership team to be

responsible for leading the school's behaviour improvement strategy alongside a systematic professional development programme for all staff.

- Staff trained to enable children to understand good nutrition, and its benefits to health and well-being.
- Schools to comply with the Race Relations Amendment Act 2000 and DfES guidance relating to analysing exclusion levels of ethnic groups.
- The requirement to notify parents in writing of exclusion enhanced to inform them of their responsibilities.
- Reintegration interviews to be mandatory following any fixed period of exclusion from a primary or special school, and of over five days in a secondary school.
- Schools to provide work for all periods of exclusion.
- Schools, through constructive dialogue, to agree local arrangements for behaviour support.
- School collaborations to encourage managed transfers of pupils on the principle of 'one pupil out, one pupil in'.
- Schools to offer parenting contracts prior to exclusion to tackle poor behaviour at school.
- The power to apply for a parenting order extended to schools following serious misbehaviour at school.
- Wherever possible, all secondary school children to have access to a learning support unit among the local partnership of schools.
- Learning support units to complement other provision in schools and not be used as a dumping ground for misbehaving children but attempt to improve behaviour and support continued learning.
- All schools to ensure pupil and parent support in order to meet the objectives of *Every Child Matters* by the establishment in all schools by September 2007 of a pupil parent support worker (PPSW).

The summary and the full report can be accessed through http://tinyurl.com/ayxaw. However, as you can see, a number of these recommendations involve parental involvement and it is to this area that we now turn.

The Role of Parents

As mentioned in Chapter 5, parents remain the greatest influence on their children and there is strong evidence that establishing partnerships with parents enhances pupils' learning abilities. Information from the DfES encourages effective partnership between schools and parents and states that 'parents are children's first and most enduring educators'.

When parents and practitioners work together, the results have a positive impact on the child's development and learning. All settings should therefore seek to develop partnerships with parents, particularly in those areas where partnerships might have been resisted in the past.

Parental involvement in schools results in:

- improved pupil attainment and ownership
- increased understanding and participation by parents of their child's education
- increased opportunities for adults to enhance their own leaning
- improved ability of the school to act as a focus and a facility for the community.

Research indicates that while some parents may feel involved in their child's learning, genuine equality in partnership rarely exists.

A number of models have been designed for parent–school interaction; for example, those from Cunningham and Davis (1985):

- The **expert model** – where the parent passively receives advice and wisdom from the school.
- The **transplant model** – where skills are passed between the school and the parent.
- The **consumer model** – where there is an equal state of knowledge and the rights of the parents are recognized.

However, it is likely that relationships between school staff and parents do not fit exactly into any of these models, but show characteristics of more than one of them. The key issue is that of developing partnerships with parents in order to provide a two-way flow of information, knowledge and expertise. Common features of effective practice should include the following:

- staff showing respect for the role of parents in their child's education
- the past and future part played by parents in the education of their children being recognized and encouraged
- staff listening to parents' account of their child's development and taking action to address concerns they have
- ensuring that parents feel welcome and valued through provision of a range of opportunities for collaboration between children, parents and practitioners
- use by the school of a variety of ways to keep parents informed about the curriculum, such as brochures, displays and videos, which are made available in the parents' home language
- opportunities to talk with staff and record information about progress and achievements
- relevant learning opportunities being shared with home, and home experiences being used to promote learning.

In all of these the key element is that the parents should feel involved and valued as partners in their child's education. However, some Government initiatives have given less positive messages to parents regarding their role with schools. Formalized school links such as the development of home–school agreements and homework contracts suggest a legal responsibility that few parents welcome, particularly those whom the school might wish to influence most. The recent media coverage of the granting to headteachers power to fine the parents of children who truant places schools on the opposite side to parents and threatens the development of the trust and sharing necessary for working together.

Although recent policies such as the Respect agenda are aimed at anti-social behaviour across the UK and not specifically in schools, parents are put very much 'in the dock' as one of the main groups to be targeted. One suggestion is developing a national parenting academy to coach parents on how to control their children, this being alongside proposals giving the police the powers for round-the-clock supervision of the most difficult problem families, with the option to remove the worst-offending families to 'sin bin' residential units. Furthermore, legislation is also expected to expand the number of organizations and agencies which can apply for parenting orders, as well as providing for fines for the parents of excluded pupils who are found unsupervised during school hours without reasonable excuse.

Draconian as the above provisions might sound, emphasis on parental responsibility is not just a Government idea but is a reflection of the views held by many teachers. In 2001 questionnaires were send to 2,000 members of the Association of Teachers and Lecturers, 1,000 each to primary and secondary teachers. A total of 47 per cent of these were returned and they revealed that:

- 88 per cent thought that unless parental support for learning increased, the Government's aim to raise standards would not be met
- 51 per cent thought that SATs did not help parents understand more about their child's learning
- 67 per cent thought that the majority of parents want to help their child's learning but do not know how best to do so
- 72 per cent thought that the legal obligations of parents for their child's education should extend further than at present.

It was also found that many parents appear to share the most commitment towards school when their children are at their youngest. Attendance in early years settings necessitates regular face-to-face contact with staff as parents deliver and collect children. However, as children become more independent, the gap grows, and in some schools, due to concerns relating to staff and pupil safety, parents are actively discouraged from entering school premises. A primary headteacher recently told me that the parents are only really involved up to the end of Key Stage 1: 'Once they get into Years 4 and 5 you never see them . . . they think that discipline is our job.'

In a research project undertaken by the Institute of Public Policy Research (IPPR) in association with Wednesbury Education Action Zone, the initial questionnaire indicated that 25 per cent of the parents who responded agreed with the statement 'A child's education is the sole responsibility of the school'. This is a perception that needs to be challenged. The report indicated that reasons for non-involvement could include:

- lack of confidence
- lack of knowledge
- other commitments
- relationship between parents and child
- many parents were content with the present situation and thought additional involvement with school unnecessary.

To increase parental involvement in school requires additional opportunities for positive and informal interaction between parents and school staff. This cannot be achieved easily. With the present pressure upon time in school, additional liaison with parents seems unlikely to increase without careful and determined planning.

Improving Links with Parents
Success in the education of children will depend in part on the involvement of a child's parents. If a child sees that their parents place a high priority upon education they are far more likely to view their schooling in a positive light and be more receptive to learning.

Therefore, to encourage effective pupil learning and school success, parents should be viewed as vital partners in a child's education. Not only can they help in ensuring homework is handed in on time and in giving coaching and advice out of school hours, but they also determine the child's home environment, where children spend much of their waking hours. As a result, engaging and working with parents is a vital part of providing children with an education that will allow them to reach their potential.

Although no magic formula exists to achieve these objectives, the following suggestions may prove helpful.

- Asking parents what they expect from the school, so as to encourage ownership and sharing of responsibility.
- Making clear what the school expects of parents and how it will support them in meeting such expectations.
- Using devices such as independent audits to obtain information on what parents think of the school and then acting on any concerns raised.
- Assessing the effectiveness of action aimed at increasing the involvement of parents and then deciding upon whether additional action is needed to increase the participation any specific parent groups.
- Gathering information to identify any obstacles to parental involvement and taking action to reduce their impact.
- Assessing the impact of multi-agency collaboration in building effective working relationships with hard-to-reach parents.
- Providing accessible information on how parents can help their child and ensuring that a non-judgemental and consistent message is delivered.
- Increasing staff awareness of the importance of involving parents, and identifying ways to increase their ability and opportunity to interact with parents.
- Listening to the views of pupils on reasons why parents do not involve themselves with education and then formulating action in an attempt to rectify the situation.
- Ensuring that main entrances are clearly signposted so that parents do not experience difficulty finding their way to the reception office.

- Assessing the impact of language used on signs and its suitability to welcome parents. Are the school's signs written in positive language? For example, 'All visitors must report to the school office' can be changed to 'Welcome to .... School. Please report to Reception.'
- Ensuring that school receptionists have received training on welcoming parents, are informative, and have the time to listen to parent enquiries and respond.
- Checking that there is an effective procedure for ensuring that all written and telephone enquiries from parents are dealt with promptly.
- Providing a variety of forms of communication to contact parents. For example, telephone and school websites could be used to convey good news and celebrate pupil success.
- Considering the appointment, even part-time, of a home–school liaison officer whose brief is to increase parental involvement, or increasing positive use of educational welfare officers to build bridges between home and school.
- Reviewing the quality and appearance of written home–school communication to ensure it does impact positively upon parental involvement.
- Consideration of devices such as 'mail merge' to personalize letters to parents.
- Ensuring that signatures on letters to parents include forenames to reinforce the equality of the partnership with parents.
- Improving the information given to parents on what pupils are taught in order to increase their ability to enhance their child's learning and interest.
- If parents are expected to encourage or help their children's learning at home, considering how they can be supported by the school to do this.
- Welcoming the diversity of parents and encouraging drawing on such diversity so as to increase specific areas of knowledge or expertise.

- Promoting family learning or family fun activities that provide an opportunity for staff and parents to mix in a less formal environment.
- Identifying parental needs and interests in order to provide support programmes.
- Ensuring that all staff place equal value on all parents, irrespective of background or ability.

12 Resilience of Students and Staff

Resilience of Students

There is no doubt that despite some of the factors that can contribute to challenging behaviour and despite the difficulties that some children face, many display amazing resilience.

Resilience is a term that describes the ability to resist what are usually negative influences or factors that can make it less likely that individuals achieve specific levels of well-being. To a certain extent resilience is the guardian angel to offset the pressure of the risk elements outlined in Chapter 1. Although no single definition exists, resilience appears to involve several related elements. First, a sense of self-esteem and confidence; second, a belief in one's own self-efficacy and ability to deal with change and adaptation, and third, a repertoire of social problem-solving approaches. As with risk factors, features that serve to reduce the impact of risk or promote resilience relate to characteristics within the child, family or wider community and can include any combination of these factors.

Resilience factors in the child

- Secure early relationships
- Being female
- Higher intelligence
- Easy temperament when an infant
- Positive attitude, problem-solving approach
- Good communication skills
- A planner, belief in control

- Humour
- Religious faith
- Capacity to reflect.

Resilience factors in the family
- At least one good parent–child relationship
- Affection
- Clear, firm and consistent discipline
- Support for education
- Supportive, long-term relationship, absence of severe discord.

Resilience factors in the community

- Wider supportive network
- Good housing
- High standard of living
- A high-morale school with a positive attitude generally, and positive policies on behaviour and on anti-bullying
- Schools with strong academic as well as non-academic opportunities
- A range of positive sport/leisure facilities.

Within this range, however, specific themes appear to be vital, including positive relationships with peers. This particular issue suggests the need to obtain and maintain skills in interaction and communication in an environment that values all, provides equality of opportunity, where bullying or isolation are rejected and all see themselves as having a responsibility for each other's well-being. The teaching of social skills needs to underline other activities and be rehearsed through drama activities and through assembly, discussion and reflection. Effective and supportive interaction needs to be modelled to the pupils through positive adult-to-adult, and adult-to-child, interaction.

Other key issues include considering realistic future plans. Children may verbalize ideas for the future that are not based on their experience and abilities but instead on ambitious dreams that have little chance of being achieved. They are then disappointed when their plans are unfulfilled. Children who have been supported too closely may have acquired an assumed helplessness and wait for others to take decisions and actions on their behalf. Teaching children to develop independence and to rely on themselves to identify and solve problems, to take small achievable steps towards all targets, gives them control and supports increased self-esteem.

Having a positive sense of being able to achieve and deal effectively with tasks is also important but can only be developed if pupils believe that in some area of their life they can attain at a level that has value to themselves and others. Schools that place a focus upon recognition of all skills – creative, social and academic – have the best chance of ensuring that children feel they are likely to achieve recognition. Encouraging children to see value in themselves and in others is a vital part of this process.

Finally, and most importantly, possessing a strong attachment with at least one adult will be central to success. Often it is taken for granted that a child has at least one adult that he or she relies upon and can trust but for some this may not be the case. Teachers and teaching assistants may fill this gap, but the distance that professionals need to maintain may well result in the schools considering the option of mentors to provide an anchor for those at risk. Also the role of youth workers should not be underestimated as they too can provide security. Increasing school and youth club staff interaction through ventures such as joint training and joint initiatives may increase the value of this contact.

Children above all else need positive adult role models – in my opinion nothing is more important in the quest to manage challenging behaviour.

Resilience of Staff

So, who is going to look after the role models? They need support, too. How are they to remain resilient and what does it take to survive the rigours of this responsibility and to stay sane?

Although much has been written about the effects of poor behaviour depressing morale and increasing the stress felt by teachers and those involved in multi-agency approaches, including health and child care services, many in the field remain both positive and committed to their role.

Although many reasons are cited as to why teachers still enjoy their job, it appears that two main factors are crucial. They are:

1   The specific culture of the school and the colleagues that you work with.
2   Their own ability to deal with the stresses and strains of the role.

Though issues such as pay and conditions are important, the most important issue appears to be the role of the senior management of the school to develop a positive learning culture and to support and back up their staff.

What really struck a chord with me was the observation by Barclay in a *Times Educational Supplement* article in 2005 that in order to try to reach the objectives of *Every Child Matters* we really need to establish the culture that 'Every Teacher Matters' too. To achieve this state of affairs Barclay highlighted the following six key areas:

- staff welfare
- empowerment of all staff
- simple systems
- using staff strengths
- creating a no-blame culture
- being positive and optimistic.

Though most of the above are obvious, it is worth repeating again the last two, which are a no-blame culture and remaining positive and optimistic.

It is vital that we let staff express themselves, use their expertise and experience, and that we let them trust their instincts. I believe teachers need to take calculated risks in managing challenging behaviour. Backing staff to make such decisions, and being supportive, is so important, as is developing a culture in which it is recognized that mistakes will and invariably must happen if behavioural objectives are to be achieved.

Having made this point, some of the other factors in achieving resilience among individual staff members will depend on one's own threshold of tolerance and stress.

Although stress is such a relative term, it is usually influenced by the 3Cs which are:

- *Control* – sense of purpose and direction
- *Commitment* – to work, but also hobbies, social life and families
- *Challenge* – seeing changes as normal and positive, rather than a threat.

In evaluating stress, the following warning signs should be heeded.

Own general behaviour

- inability to sleep
- emotional outbursts
- excessive eating/drinking
- difficulty concentrating
- forgetfulness
- driving aggressively (yes, really!)
- forgetfulness (look it appears again . . .!)
- indecisiveness

One's body

- high blood pressure
- tenseness
- backache
- difficulty breathing

Emotions

- depression
- guilt

- moodiness
- jealousy
- anxieties

In addition, although earlier on we mentioned students' anger as being a feature of your role in managing behaviour, it is important to manage your own anger and frustrations and to remember that anger is a natural, healthy and emotional response when you feel threatened. It is also important to recognize that bottling up feelings of anger can be unhealthy not just for you but for those with whom you work and for your family.

Long and Vizard (2002) in their booklet *Behaviour Matters*, suggest the following in order to help control the anger that might be felt by teachers working in the field of challenging behaviour:

- practice relaxation techniques, deep breathing, count to five
- depersonalize the situation'
- keep an anger diary and identify what triggers anger
- own your anger . . . say out loud what makes you angry
- reframe the problem, try to look at situations as both challenges and opportunities
- be assertive and say 'no' if you think demands on your time are unreasonable.

Regarding the last point, do say 'no', or delegate, if you are not sure whether you have the time or skills to do something. Though not always possible, it is sometimes essential to say 'no' to people who are overloading you. In my experience, teachers say yes far too often.

Some teachers really find delegation a problem. They try to do everything themselves and while this is laudable they will burn out unless they develop the skill to delegate. Advice regarding delegation includes:

- choose tasks to delegate which free you to undertake planning
- be clear about outcomes, deadlines and budgets

- select people you believe have the capacity to complete or learn to do the task
- give people authority to choose how they do the task
- support by coaching and mentoring
- during and upon completion of the task give credit to the person to whom you delegated it
- track the programme but without interfering.

Delegating responsibility involves not expecting others to complete a task without your support, and finally and most importantly, realizing that others will often handle the task in a different way than you would do, and just, perhaps, may not do it as well as you would!

With regards to the job itself there will be good days and there will bad days. There will be days when you think 'Why on earth did I get into this?', but having said that, there will be days when you have some major breakthrough with a particular child or situation and you will sit back and say 'Yes, that's why I do this . . . I'm good at this'.

Will you be happy or successful in your role? Only you can answer this, but it might be worth remembering the following:

Success is getting what you want . . . happiness is liking what you get
(Anon)

Student Behaviour Profiles

When working with difficult, demanding and defiant students, it is sometimes impossible to know what approach is the best to take. An old Chinese proverb states that 'the longest journey starts with the first step'. In the case of troubleshooting challenging behaviours of specific students, one of the first steps could be to develop a Student Behaviour Profile.

Profiling can achieve two main aims:

1 To focus on one or two specific areas to be addressed.
2 To establish if any pattern exists and identify antecedents or triggers.

Options for management of challenging behaviour can be discussed in the form of practical measures which may include some or all of the following:

- Management of rewards and sanctions
- Curriculum differentiation
- Management systems for non-structured time
- Looking at alternative skills pathways
- Considering alternative treatments
- Working with multi-agencies
- School support programmes.

The following five cases reflect students profiled by a group of teachers over the period 2002 to 2005 during INSET sessions run throughout the UK. In all cases the teachers did not write down their own thoughts but reviewed them with a partner who acted as their scribe. Note that in the first three cases the management ideas presented reflect my own thoughts in conjunction with ideas presented on the day. In the last two cases the ideas presented were the result of a 20-minute group discussion between fellow professionals during INSET sessions. These discussions comprised a group of five or six professionals including teachers, teaching assistants and multi-agency workers. I have, however, added some comments regarding their management strategies. In all cases the names of the students have been changed but I believe many of the issues outlined will be familiar to teachers in schools throughout the world.

Student Profile 1

Outline the key behavioural issues of a specific child that you are working with at present and then complete the questions below:

Name of child: *Kyle*   Age: *12*   Sex: *Male*

What is your relationship to this child? *Classroom Teacher*

Now complete the Student Profile by answering the following questions:

- Which issues, learning or behavioural, are the major cause for concern? Be specific.
  Aggressive, Attention seeker

- In what situations do the issues raised above occur? (i.e. in what settings/context, with or without other students involved)
  When asked to do something he does not want to do and in any situation with or without others

- In which situations do the issues not occur?
  When he is happy to do what he has been asked but will do this one day and not others

- What skills does the student generate? (i.e. social/communication skills or learning/curriculum skills).
  Is good at art and IT but does not always finish assigned work in these classes

- What view does the student have of himself/herself?
  Does not see his behaviour as a problem

- What are the views of other students?
  They are fed up with him and as a result he has no close friends

- Is the curriculum offered appropriate for this student?
  No, as he really appears to be a kinaesthetic style of learner

- What is the situation with regards to the parents?
  Reluctant to be involved, they think he is the school's problem when he is there

Management options

In the case of Kyle what we first need to establish is what is the message behind the behaviour exhibited.

At first sight he appears to be a classic case of an aggressive young man finding the transition to secondary school difficult. However, it is likely that from the profile outlined that he is probably struggling to actually access the curriculum, probably because he may have difficulties with basic skills. It looks as if he can't do the work and because of a lack of positive support at home he now does not want to try.

As a result we need to develop a series of short-term and long-term range options to coax him back into a more proactive mode of wanting to try to overcome his difficulties while also getting his parents involved whether they see this as their role or not.

SHORT-TERM

- Differentiated curriculum.
- Change of class . . . fresh start, possibly new Tutor Group.
- Meeting with parents to discuss Behaviour Action Contract and Peer Mentor.
- 'Time out' non-verbal action cards issued to Kyle.
- Some possible time scheduled in the learning support unit.

LONG-TERM

- Assessment for Specific Learning Difficulties.
- Counselling to assess reasons for frustration.
- Look into activities to channel aggression, i.e. martial arts.
- Work in IT or Art assigned and related to a longer-term project, perhaps with a local business or school magazine production.

Summary

The key element here is getting Kyle to feel better about himself and for his parents to engage in this process. A fresh start in a new class along with the focus provided by the BAC is essential. In addition I believe that he needs help with his learning difficulties and more proactive outlets for his aggression in order to provide a framework for success.

Student Profile 2

Think of a specific child who you know to be struggling at present and then complete the questions below:

Name of child: *Ashley*   Age: *10*   Sex: *Female*

What is your relationship to this child? *Headteacher*

Now complete the Student Profile by answering the following questions:

- Which issues, learning or behavioural, are the major cause for concern? Be specific.
  Violent outbursts. No knowledge of outbursts after event

- In what situations do the issues raised above occur? (i.e. in what settings/context, with or without other students involved)
  Anywhere. Usually involves peer or adult

- In which situations do the issues not occur?
  Occurs in all situations. No pattern

- What skills does the student generate? (i.e. social/communication skills or learning/curriculum skills).
  Verbally very articulate and likes to be in charge

- What view does the student have of himself/herself?
  Thinks she is bad, knows she has an anger problem. Does not realize the impact because she can't remember the issues correctly

- What are the views of other students?
  Frightened, no close friends

- Is the curriculum offered appropriate for this student?
  Yes

- What is the situation with regards to the parents?
  Supportive but depressed

Management options

In the case of Ashley the most interesting aspect is that she does not appear to remember the outbursts after the event, which is something that needs to be investigated by specific professionals.

The key here will be to help her train herself to channel her aggression in some other way, and I feel that careful mood management will be the main issue to be addressed by all that supervise her in group situations.

SHORT-TERM

- A Mood Card system implemented for both Supervisors and Ashley for Time Out or Calm Down time.
- Options to help her concentrate in class such as tangle toys, bar magnets, etc.
- Responsibly roles for Ashley created in classroom and break time situations – perhaps helping with lower age group.
- Behaviour Action Contract with target to be agreed in connection with her anger management issues and regular contact with parents regarding progress.
- Study Buddy assigned in the classroom.

LONG-TERM

- Multi-agency assessment to assess anger issues and lack of recall thereafter.
- Possible filming of events or otherwise developing a role-play situation to illustrate the impact of her actions to her.
- All staff trained to recognize key early warning signs in her mood changes.
- Circle Time used to break down some of the barriers between her and other students in the group.

Summary

Ashley could well be a student with ADHD and ODD due to some of the patterns of her behaviour, and as a result the key element here would be a referral towards an assessment. This possibility is further enhanced by both her lack of memory after an event and as her parents also appear to be struggling with the situation.

Self-esteem however and trying to generate positive experiences with other individuals is crucial and therefore using her skills with helping in the classroom and with younger students will be important factors.

Student Profile 3

Think of a specific child who you know is struggling at present and then complete the questions below:

Name of child: *Jamie*   Age: *8*   Sex: *Male*

What is your relationship to this child? *Classroom teacher*

Now complete the Student Profile by answering the following questions:

- Which issues, learning or behavioural, are the major cause for concern? Be specific
  Very bright, reading age 11 years, but task avoidance for written work. Physically aggressive to peers and defiant behaviour

- In what situations do the issues raised above occur? (i.e. in what settings/context, with or without other students involved)
  When class is noisy, when asked to do something, in unstructured situations

- In which situations do the issues not occur?
  When he is following his own agenda and the centre of attention

- What skills does the student generate? (i.e. social/communication skills or learning/curriculum skills).
  Good reader, good comprehension, strong verbal skills and very engaging in 1–1 situations with adults

- What view does the student have of himself/herself?
  Wants to please but doesn't take responsibility for his actions

- What are the views of other students?
  No real friends, peers reluctant to visit home

- Is the curriculum offered appropriate for this student?
  Yes but doesn't always finish tasks given

- What is the situation with regards to the parents?
  Very anxious and involved but possible questions of poor attachment and management

Management options

For Jamie the classroom is simply too busy as he is easily distracted and this in effect is upsetting his equilibrium. I think the key area to cover here is that Jamie actually will need to be distracted but in a more structured way.

SHORT-TERM

- Work station created where he works independently for up to two hours a day.
- Individual project work devised for him during part of this time along with more independent time for written assignments.
- Allowing him to wear a headset during this time containing music of his choice.
- Behaviour Action Contract with the target related to work production but with the emphasis 'not to lay hands on any other pupil'. If this continues sanctions to be created to include time with headteacher at the end of the day.
- Daily contact with parents established through the BAC.

LONG-TERM

- Friendship group established for Jaime at school, possibly started at break time through an activity club.
- Possibly parents invited into the school and encouraged to join the school PTA in order to establish links with other parents.

Summary

Jamie needs to be stretched both academically and nurtured carefully socially. From the profile notes there is a possibility that he could be Gifted and both his skills and weaknesses will probably need more independent teaching. For this reason I believe the use of the work station should be encouraged for this situation.

Having said this I believe we need to be very firm about the aggression displayed in this case and if this continues then time with the head or deputy should take place. It is to be hoped however that concentrating on the positive aspects of work completion in the BAC will help to offset this behaviour both in the short and long term.

Developing more positive relationships between Jamie and other pupils will require two points of attack: friendship groups in school, and by encouraging his parents to meet other parents to develop opportunities for this to happen outside of the school hours.

Student Profile 4

Think of a specific child who you know to be presently struggling with learning in the school and then complete the questions below:

Name of child: *Nigel*   Age: *13*   Sex: *Male*

What is your relationship to this child? *Head of year*

Now complete the Student Profile by answering the following questions:

- Which issues, learning or behavioural, are the major cause for concern? Be specific
  Argues with staff about anything

- In what situations does the issue raised above occur? (i.e. in what settings/context, with or without other students involved)
  Most lessons, lunchtime, break

- In which situations do the issues not occur?
  Earlier in the day is better

- What skills does the student generate? (i.e. social/communication skills or learning/curriculum skills).
  Creative with drawing

- What view does the student have of himself/herself?
  No acceptance

- What are the views of other students?
  His poor behaviour is viewed as normal

- Is the curriculum offered appropriate for this student?
  We cannot offer any other

- What is the situation with regards to the parents?
  Not interested, told by Dad he doesn't want him

Management options
SHORT-TERM
- Shortened lunchtimes may help – not so hyped up.
- Attach mentor to him.
- Withdraw from different lessons.
- Modify timetable, i.e. after lunch special timetable.

- BEST involvement with parents.
- Modified timetable alternative Year 10.

Comments on Action

The overall flavour by the teacher from whose comments were made for the Profile appeared that they were frustrated with Nigel – and let's face it some of these kids will drive you to drink. As the head of year the teacher involved is probably inundated with complaints on a daily basis and as a result it is probably likely that it is not the case that this happens in most lessons but that it just seems to. Also the comment about not being able to offer any alternative curriculum seems to emphasize the hole that everyone thinks they are in with this child.

The suggestions by the teaching group appear to identify this as there are classes that do appear to work for him and the suggestion about being withdrawn from certain classes is something that should *not* be seen as avoidance of certain staff or courses but as a device to build up some positive experiences in the programme at this time.

The relationship at home does not look productive and as a result the idea about using a learning mentor is a very good idea, and counselling if available could also be considered. Further to this the idea of more proactive approaches with regards to lunchtimes and with the afternoon timetable shows clear signs of flexible thinking on behalf of the group.

It is true that in order to engage the parents the involvement of a multi-agency team such as BEST (Behaviour and Education Support Team) is a good idea and further to this it may also be an idea for Social Services to be notified.

As he appears talented with drawing I also wonder if this area could be further explored. Students like Nigel are often interested in areas such as graphic design and advertising. Computer programmes can be used to support this interest area as well looking at local services in this field for work study placements, especially in Year 10.

Overall we need to break the negative cycle that he appears to be in at this time.

Student Profile 5

Think of a specific child who you know to be presently struggling with learning in the school and then complete the questions
below:

Name of child: *Tom*   Age: *15*   Sex: *Male*

What is your relationship to this child? *SENCO*

Now complete the Student Profile by answering the fol-
lowing questions:

- Now list the main issues of concern, be specific, and not
  more than 5.
  *Will not comply with any requests, very defiant. Refuses to do any-
  thing unless on his terms*

- In what situations does the issue raised above occur? (i.e. in what
  settings/context, with or without other students involved)
  *All the time, whenever he thinks he is in a situation where he feels
  he might fail. Or when he has his own agenda*

- In which situations do the issues not occur?
  Better when he is one to one with no other pupils around. No pressure

- What skills does the student generate? (i.e. social/communi-
  cation skills or learning/curriculum skills).
  Verbally very good, also good with practical tasks

- What view does the student have of himself/herself?
  *Very low self-esteem. Very afraid of other kids finding out how weak
  he is*

- What are the views of other students?
  Annoyed by him, some dislike him, others pity him

- Is the curriculum offered appropriate for this student?
  *Statemented, literacy is very poor, better now he can go out on work
  placements*

- What is the situation with regards to the parents?
  *One-parent family, mother has four other younger children, rarely sees
  Dad*

Management options

SHORT-TERM

- Take audience away – work one on one.
- Walk away when he is being negative.
- Build relationship with one person.
- Use rewards – special privileges, able to make himself a cup of tea.
- Start afresh each time, don't carry over problems.

LONG-TERM

- Arrange IEP to maintain key targets.
- Modified timetable – reduced timetable.
- Work placement/alternative training.
- Use of alternative recording devices.
- Use of counselling/Circle Time/Circle of Friends.

Comments on action

As you will probably note the style of analysis from the SENCO is somewhat different than from the form tutor. To some extent the assessment is more positive but yet in other ways also more despairing.

The ideas presented by the group both in the short and long term show that they seem focused on trying to work on two main areas: Tom's self-esteem, and providing him with skills based future.

Both of these options I fully support due to fact that basically Tom is in my opinion a scared young man. It is likely that he will shortly have to leave the structure of school although he has struggled there to take on an outside world before coming to terms with working within a school community.

Tom as pointed out by the group really needs to have the preparation to feel better about himself and therefore providing him with as many successful experiences as possible is vital.

As a result modifying timetables and to some extent curriculum options and ways to record his thoughts and work especially at this age is important. In addition a rewards-based culture is going to be vital to establish any real momentum with this young man.

Further to this giving him options to deal with his anger

and frustration as well as possibly trying to address the potential deep-seated issues of insecurities of his home life will be best dealt with by non-teaching staff.

One area that can often assist these individuals is being given responsibility of working with younger children as a student assistant.

Having said that the pupils in his own year need to help to make Tom part of the team. Whether they mean to or not they are bullying him despite the fact he may be a provocative victim.

Conclusion

In this book I have attempted to cover many aspects of challenging behaviours and what to do about them.

In so many ways the issues raised by challenging behaviour are a challenge to the very essence of school life in terms of not just providing children with academic and social skills but in the basic requirements of safety and security.

Do schools reflect society, or does society reflect our schools? This is obviously a question for debate and one on which opinions will differ. One opinion on why we now seem to have more problems recently appeared on the internet in the form of a lament to days long past:

> Today we mourn the passing of a beloved old friend, Common Sense, who has been with us for many years. No one knows for sure how old he was since his birth records were long ago lost in red tape.
>
> He will be remembered as having cultivated such valuable lessons as life isn't always fair, and maybe it was my fault.
>
> Common Sense lived by simple and reliable parenting strategies (adults, not children, are in charge).
>
> His health began to deteriorate rapidly when well-intentioned but overbearing regulations were set in place.
>
> Reports of a six-year-old boy charged with sexual harassment for kissing a classmate; teens suspended from school for using mouthwash after lunch; and a teacher fired for reprimanding an unruly student, only worsened his condition.
>
> Common Sense lost ground when parents attacked teachers for doing the job they failed to do in disciplining their unruly children.
>
> It declined even further when schools were required to get parental

consent to administer Panadol, sun lotion or a sticky plaster to a student; but, could not inform the parents when a student became pregnant and wanted to have an abortion.

Common Sense was preceded in death by his parents, Truth and Trust; his wife, Discretion; his daughter, Responsibility; and his son, Reason. He is survived by three stepbrothers; I Know My Rights, Someone Else is to Blame, and I'm A Victim.

(Anon)

This lament makes the point that things were better in the past: but who knows for sure that this is so.

There is obviously no single solution to managing challenging behaviour but some possible answers have been highlighted in this book, and of course, we have explored one specific Behaviour Management Model, courtesy of the 'Scottish teacher' principle. It appears the Scottish invented almost everything from Radar to steam engines, so perhaps they should be credited with engineering the definitive Behaviour Management Model as well.

Whatever the origins of challenging behaviour, Structure and Flexibility, supported by Respect, Relationships and Role Models, are key terms in teaching and management.

Finally, I came upon this list of wise observations that some little children have learned by their experience in dealing with adults:

Great truths of little children

- No matter how hard you try, you can't baptize cats.
- When your Mum is mad at your Dad, don't let her brush your hair.
- If your sister hits you, don't hit her back. They always catch the second person.
- Never ask your 4-year-old brother to hold a tomato.
- You can't trust dogs to watch your food.
- Don't sneeze when someone is cutting your hair.
- Never hold a dust buster and a cat at the same time.

- You can't hide a piece of broccoli in a glass of milk.
- Don't wear polka-dot underwear under white shorts.
- The best place when you're sad is Grandpa's lap.

Amen to these!

References

Biddulph, S. (1997) *Raising Boys.* Harper Collins.

Briers, A. (2004) *Safer School Communities.* Middlesex University Press.

Cooper, P. and O'Regan, F. (2001) *Educating Children with ADHD.* Routledge Falmer.

Dunn, P. (2004) *Acceptable Behaviour Contracts.* Metropolitan Police Press.

Dunn, R. (2005) *Do's and Don'ts of Behaviour Management.* Continuum.

Goldberg, S. (2005) *Ready to Learn.* Oxford University Press.

Griffiths, G. (2002) *Managing Boys' Behaviour.* Hawker Brownlow Education.

Kewley, G. (1999) *ADHD Recognition, Reality and Resolution.* LAC Press.

Olsen, J. and Cooper, P. (2001) *Dealing with Disruptive Students.* Kogan Page.

O'Regan, F. (2002) *How To Teach and Manage Children with ADHD.* LDA.

O'Regan, F. (2005) *ADHD.* Continuum.

O'Regan, F. (2005) *Surviving and Succeeding with SEN.* Continuum.

Long, R. (2000) *Making Sense of Behaviour.* NASEN.

Long, R. and Vizard, D. (2002) *Behaviour Matters.* Rob Long.

Steer, A. (2006) *Learning Behaviour Report.* DfES.

Train, A. (1995) *The Bullying Problem.* London Souvenir Press.

Index